Perfect Phrases for Law School Acceptance

Perfect Phrases for Law School Acceptance

Hundreds of Ready-to-Use Phrases to Write a Winning Personal Statement, Ace the Interview, and Impress Admissions Officers

Paul Bodine

New York Chicago San Francisco Lisbon London
Madrid Mexico City Milan New Delhi San Juan
Seoul Singapore Sydney Toronto

1 2 3 4 5 6 7 8 9 0   DOC/DOC   0 1 4 3 2 1 0 9 8

ISBN 978-0-07-159822-4
MHID   0-07-159822-7

This book is printed on acid-free paper.

McGraw-Hill books are available at special quantity discounts for use as premiums and sales promotions, or for use in corporate training programs. For more information, please write to the Director of Special Sales, McGraw-Hill Professional, Two Penn Plaza, New York, NY, 10121 – 2298. Or contact your local bookstore.

This publication is designed to provide accurate and authoritative information in regard to the subject matter covered. It is sold with the understanding that neither the author nor the publisher is engaged in rendering legal, accounting, or other professional services. If legal advice or other expert assistance is required, the services of a competent professional person should be sought.

> —*From a Declaration of Principles jointly adopted*
> *By a Committee of the American Bar*
> *Association and a Committee of Publishers.*

Note: All the examples used in this book are fictional. The names of actual organizations and individuals have been used only for illustrative purposes and are not intended to represent or characterize the actual organizations and individuals.

Library of Congress Cataloging-in-Publication Data

Bodine, Paul, 1959-
    Perfect phrases for law school acceptance : hundreds of ready-to-use phrases to write a winning personal statement, ace the interview, and impress admissions officers / Paul Bodine.
        p. cm.
    Includes bibliographical references and index.
    ISBN-13: 978-0-07-159822-4 (acid-free paper)
    ISBN-10: 0-07-159822-7 (acid-free paper) 1. Law schools—United States—Admission. 2. Essay—Authorship. 3. College applications—United States. I. Title.
    KF285.B63 2008
    340.071'173—dc22   2008020242

For Sid and Naomi

Contents

Contents

Contents

Preface

The Juris Doctor (JD) is a powerful, versatile, well-remunerated degree—and an increasingly popular one. Today the world's most selective law schools know they'll receive enough applications boasting outstanding "numbers" (grades and LSATs) to populate multiple entering classes. For that very reason, they can afford to assemble not only the most intellectually capable class, but also the one whose sheer variety and distinctiveness is most likely to create the synergies that make education more than a merely academic experience. For each of the following applicant types, the personal statement (and supporting written documents) will likely be a deciding factor in the law schools' decision to accept or reject:

- *Applicants applying to top schools:* Test scores and grades are so stratospheric that essays become the best way to distinguish the special from the merely great.

- *Applicants from underrepresented minority groups:* Essays enable these applicants to highlight their diversity qualifications.

- *Applicants who are neither presumptive admits nor rejects:* Essays give admissions committees (adcoms) the extra information they need to decide whom to admit.

- *Applicants vying for the final slots in an entering class:* Adcoms can round out their class's diversity by learning, through the essays, which applicants offer something special.
- *Applicants with unusual stories:* The personal statement is still the best medium for applicants with exceptional experiences or backgrounds to communicate their stories to the admissions committee.
- *Applicants applying to non-index-driven law schools:* The less weight a school gives to the LSAT and grades (which together give adcoms a rough numeric gauge of applicants' potential law school success), the more weight it will give the personal insights disclosed in the personal statement.
- *Applicants who have mixed predictors:* To decide whether to admit a low-LSAT/high-GPA applicant (or the reverse), adcoms often turn to the personal statement.
- *Applicants applying to safety schools:* Here essays can have a negative impact: if they're bad they could motivate an otherwise admit-ready adcom to reject or "ding" you.
- *Low-index applicants to lower-tier schools:* When adcoms must choose from among applicants whose numbers are distinctly unimpressive, the essay can tip the scale.

The bottom line is this: the personal statement, secondary essays, addenda, and interview enable the admissions committees to look beyond the application data and see the person, to get a sense not only of what the applicant has done but why he or she has done it.

Preface

It's not easy to write essays that find the sweet spot that best captures your uniqueness and potential contribution. This book's "perfect phrases" are intended to help you overcome the paralysis the blank PC screen can induce by providing sample wording you can use to bridge the gap between outline and first draft. Because generic writing is bad writing, you'll find that the phrases and examples included here are not "one-size-fits all" templates, however. They contain the concrete details—facts, names, places, numbers—that good writing always has. Feel free to use this book's perfect phrases as inspirational prompts, guides, even temporary "crutches" as you work toward a final draft that's expressed in your own words. When you reach the point where you're confident in the substance of your essays—when writer's block is no longer an issue—search for ways to turn any of the perfect phrases you've used into your own words. Both your writing and your odds of admission will benefit.

Letting this book's perfect phrases become a substitute for your own words defeats the purpose of this book and the admissions essay. Law schools don't admit applicants who sound like other applicants or who write what they think the schools want to hear. They admit real people who tell their own stories their way. Use these perfect phrases to help you do that and only that. Then your essays' phrases will truly be "perfect."

This book focuses on the law school personal statement, secondary essay topics and addenda, and basic interview question categories. Part One briefly guides you through the sometimes stressful process of writing admissions essays, from selecting your themes, developing your raw material, and preparing an initial outline to writing, revising, and editing your drafts. Part Two provides perfect phrases for the seven most common types of essays—about your personal life, upbringing or background; challenges and disadvantages; values or beliefs; accomplishments; interests or passions; the diversity you can contribute to your class; and your career and post-J.D. goals. Two chapters also focus specifically on perfect phrases for starting and concluding essays. All the written documents that you may have to submit in addition to the personal statement and essays—from addenda, conduct (or character and fitness) statements, and transfer essays to master of laws (LLM) essays, letters of recommendation, and wait-list letters—are the subject of Part Three. Part Four provides perfect phrases for the law school admissions interview.

It's my hope that the range and variety of examples in this book will help you to unlock the creativity and inner voice that are still the surest way to spark the admission reader's interest. If you have any suggestions for improving it, please e-mail them to me at paulbodine@live.com.

Acknowledgments

My thanks to Anya Kozorez of McGraw-Hill for bringing this book about. Special thanks to Alexander Ritchie; Sherynn Perry Esq. and the Perry Law Firm PLLC; and to Karen Lundquist and Lundquist and Lange LLC. My biggest debt of gratitude is to my wife, Tamami, for her patience and support during this book's gestation.

Part I

Getting Started

Chapter 1 Writing Law School Personal Statements and Essays

A s intimidating as they can be, law school admissions essays offer you a crucial, irreplaceable advantage: they are perhaps the one component of your application over which you have the greatest control. From the themes you choose to encompass your personal "profile" and the stories you pick to illustrate them, to the lessons you draw and the tone you adopt, law schools give you, through the essays, the reins to shape how they perceive your candidacy. Helping you structure and manage the potentially frustrating and time-consuming challenge of essay writing is the subject of this chapter.

[handwritten annotations: "make fearful" above "intimidating"; "include ; surround" above "encompass"; "limit or keep under control" beside "reins to"]

Your Profile and Themes

Before you begin writing your admissions essays, you should first develop a short self-marketing message or "profile" that integrates the key themes (strengths, experiences, interests) you want your application to communicate. Take your time. Cast your net widely, and ask friends and family for their input. You want to isolate the handful of themes or experiences—from your childhood, interests, or travels to your education, career, or community life—that will best distinguish you from other applicants. This profile is the guiding message that should inform all of your law school essays and indeed your entire application, from recommendation letters to addenda to the interview. When your application pool's grades, test scores, and demographics have all been sorted and batched, this message is the one that will enable your application to stand out from the pack.

Data Mining Your Life

Once you have nailed down your themes, you need to identify the individual stories to build each essay around. You can do this by "data mining" your experiences through conversations with family and friends, résumé-based brainstorming, or "stream-of-consciousness" writing (aka the "brain dump").

If you've done it right, your data-mining process should leave you with a mass of raw material that could fill dozens of personal statements. Now you need to evaluate your raw stories critically. Continually ask yourself which of the possible essay stories have the most value or significance. A story's external significance could include its impact on your life (such as an academic honor or promotion) or on others' lives (such as helping teens earn A's as a mentor). A story's internal significance would include how the experience changed you, enhanced your skills, deepened your perspective, strengthened your sense of your potential, and so on. It may be true, for example, that your leadership is amply illustrated by your captaincy of your college track team. But because athletics is a fairly common admissions essay theme and the reason you want a law degree is to be an advocate for the homeless, the better leadership story for your personal statement may be your organization of a Christmas meals event for homeless people.

Look for stories that capture in microcosm what's essential about you so you don't submit a "kitchen-sink" essay that only skims many key moments. By understanding these stories, someone can know as much about who you really are as by hearing your full autobiography. Look for the stories that are most distinctive and that combine the greatest external impact and personal transformation. If a story rates highly in distinctiveness, objective results or impact, and personal significance, you've probably got a winner. Subject all the raw stories generated by your data-mining process to this same weighing or ranking process until you've arrived at a core story or set of stories you want your personal statement (and secondary essays) to cover.

Essay Topics

How can you decide which stories will work best for each school? Unfortunately, the vast majority of law schools issue instructions that are either extremely vague or extremely all-inclusive:

- "You may write your personal statement on any subject of importance that you feel will assist us in our decision." (Georgetown)

- "There is no formula for a successful personal statement, and different individuals will find different topics to be well-suited to them. Applicants have, for example, elaborated on their significant life experiences; meaningful intellectual interests and extracurricular activities; factors inspiring them to obtain a legal education or to pursue particular career goals; significant obstacles met and overcome; special talents or skills; issues of sexual identity; particular political, philosophical, or religious beliefs; socioeconomic challenges; atypical backgrounds, educational paths, employment histories, or prior careers; or experiences and perspectives relating to disadvantage, disability, or discrimination. Any of these subjects, and many more, could be an appropriate basis for communicating important information about yourself that will aid us in reaching a thoughtful decision." (Michigan)

When you analyze the essay instructions of the top fifty-odd law schools and the essay topics that successful applicants tend to use, the following basic topic categories emerge:

- Autobiographical, personal background, and life experiences.
- Challenges and disadvantages.
- Experiences illustrating values and beliefs.
- Accomplishments.
- Passions, hobbies, and interests.
- Stories that show the diversity you can contribute to your class.
- Goals and reasons for pursuing law school.

Obviously, you cannot cover all these topics in one or even several essays. But you only need to discuss the themes that are most relevant to your profile, and that's eminently doable within the confines of a single well-crafted personal statement. This book provides perfect phrases for all these topics. Let's get started on the essays themselves.

Writing Your Essays

An outline will help you reduce the anxiety and the time drain of the writing process. By bringing structure to your personal statement before you start writing it, outlines maximize your efficiency and enable you to perform a crucial early test of the quality of your essay ideas. Do you have enough material to support your assertions or illustrate your experiences? Does the lesson or takeaway you're trying to draw from your story emerge organically from the story itself, or does it seem imposed and unearned? Outlines can help you answer these questions before you've written a draft that you're emotionally invested in.

You want to let your creativity run as you write your law school essays. At this stage, forget all the rules about transitions, "theme sentences," and "evidence sentences" that you learned in school. Even the most imaginative essays will have a basic organization, however, even if it's only the following three:

- *Introduction:* To grab the reader's attention, introduce your themes, and establish your tone.
- *Body paragraphs:* To advance your theme or narrate your story through detailed examples—the meat of your essay.

■ *Conclusion:* To reassert the essay's themes and, often, to connect the experiences presented to your future and, perhaps, to law school.

Like all good writing, your personal statement will ultimately live or die by the degree of personal, vivid detail and insight you inject into it. You want to achieve a balance between "data"—the facts that substantiate your themes—and "analysis"—that is, regularly stepping back from an example or anecdote to tell the reader what it means. Many applicants' essays never come alive on the page, and it's often because they lack specific human detail and personal anecdote. Always be as personal and concrete as you possibly can.

First Drafts

Your focus when writing the first draft of your personal statement is really just to get something down on paper. Because many applicants believe that they have to complete a polished, finished draft in the first sitting, they usually end up with a starchy, formal-sounding treatise without life or detail. Don't be so hard on yourself. Again, forget about style, grammar, and word count when you're writing your first draft. Relax, run with your outline, and don't overanalyze what you're writing—just get it down.

It may help to think of your essays as stories about an interesting and sympathetic hero—you—who's in noble pursuit of a distant and holy grail (the J.D.). People are hardwired to respond to such human-interest stories. We all like happy endings, and tales of sympathetic protagonists overcoming conflict or obstacles by changing their environment appeal to our basic hopes. Tell a good story.

Revising

Once you have written a rough draft based on your outline, step back and consider macro and organizational changes, such as contradictory themes or assertions, needlessly repeated points, gaps in context or logic, or weakly developed or poorly placed paragraphs. Continually ask yourself whether your main thesis and secondary points will be clear to the admissions readers, whether your words convey your personality and enthusiasm, whether you are telling your story as clearly, compellingly, and efficiently as you can. You may find that you need to switch around paragraphs, cut digressions, or add to, delete, or bolster your examples. Don't get stressed out. Remember, you already have your structure and rough draft; it's all downhill from here. Depending on how well-conceived your outline is and how well you fleshed it out in your first draft, your essay may go through multiple macro-level revisions before it's ready for editing proper.

Editing

The next stage, editing, means cleaning up the essay's mechanics and grammar at the sentence and word level. The potential glitches that you catch in the editing process can be everything from pronoun and subject-verb agreement, dangling modifiers, run-on sentences, and parallelism to punctuation and capitalization errors, word choice and misspelling, and active-versus passive-voice issues. One overriding rule that should guide your editing: Always choose the simplest, shortest, and most direct expression over the more complex or seemingly sophisticated one. Read your essays aloud. Do they flow? Is the tone conversational, and does it sound like you?

Your essay is finished when you can't imagine how to make it say what you mean more candidly, vividly, or directly. When you've achieved that level of honesty, color, and tautness, let go.

Part II

Perfect Phrases for Personal Statements and Secondary Essays

Chapter 2 Perfect Phrases
for Introductions

Like a smile and a firm handshake, a well-conceived introduction can create an instant positive impression on admission committee readers that may pay valuable dividends when you later need them to sympathize with a failing or sit through a not-so-compelling example. Ideally it will tell the readers what you will be accomplishing in the essay, catch and hold their interest, establish your tone, and provide some of the context or detail that creates your story's foundation. Let your themes, specific story, and creativity suggest the introduction that works best for you.

The following perfect phrases will give you some idea of the sheer variety of ways in which it's possible to open your essay:

> ■ They had found the perfect couple. Jim Webb's 2006 headquarters had asked us, the advance team for his front-porch visit to Enola, Virginia, to find a couple about to lose their health care and struggling to get by. They had to be willing to convey their struggles to

Webb before a host of cameras and reporters. When we learned the local office had found the "perfect couple," the communications director and I, the advance team press lead, drove through the winding hills of western Virginia to join the Keislers on their front porch. Jaded though I no doubt was, the story they told hit me like a body blow. Mr. Keisler had worked for 30 years at the town's small rail yard, and his wife was a hard-working school teacher. They had built a life and believed they were set for retirement. When he learned he needed heart surgery Mr. Keisler had worked right up to the surgery to ensure that he would receive his pension. When he later learned he also had prostrate cancer, he took comfort in knowing that at least his company's health insurance covered him. Then in early 2006 his former employer went bankrupt because of foreign competition and wrote off its pension liabilities. If Mr. Keisler relapsed, the couple risked losing everything they had worked for. The tears welling in Mrs. Keisler's eyes vividly reminded me of why I had joined the campaign three months before: to reset economic priorities that had gradually gone off the rails.

■ "Am I there yet?" I heard the resident ask behind the curtain. "Do you still see bone on the drill?" the physician replied matter-of-factly. Horrified, I threw a quick glance at the patient's family, who—I thanked

God—were too dazed with shock to understand what was unfolding on the other side.

- It's the early 1990s, and, as you make your way down the streets of San Francisco, a child flashes by you on a blue Schwinn. As your eyes focus on her receding form, they latch onto a vivid orange shape perched precariously on the redhead's shoulders. In all likelihood the girl you just saw was me and the passenger was a parakeet I called Tolstoy, who accompanied me on my afternoon visits to my father's office.

- It starts like any class. At ten minutes before five every Thursday afternoon, 2 professors and 22 of my fellow students and I take seats around the long tables of the poli sci department's seminar room. As everyone pulls out laptops and chats about football or weekend plans, I quietly collect myself for the role that will soon distinguish me from my undergraduate peers. At five sharp, I walk to the front of the room, stand before the words I've scrawled on the chalkboard, and begin to teach the class—my class: Model United Nations at Marquette University.

- Seeing the lights and sirens ahead, I knew the Code 415 the dispatcher had just radioed to me was about to become my first "incident." A fight had broken out on campus, culminating in a shooting and serious bodily injury. As I ran toward the half-naked teen writhing on the sidewalk, I heard Lee from Squad 2 shouting to my left, "Called it in, code 10." Just then, two shots from a porch across the intersection informed me my first crime scene was going to be much bigger than I could possibly have imagined.

- Of the 32 marines who shipped to Beirut with my father on September 15, 1982, only he and two others returned alive 17 months later.

- "Another one for the filing cabinet." After six weeks as a volunteer ranger for the Bureau of Land Management, I was beginning to learn the routine: spend hours meticulously performing field surveys of Oregon's wild mustang and spotted owl populations; prepare and present my detailed reports to my BLM supervisor; and then watch as he consigned my efforts to filing-cabinet oblivion.

- I can still remember the sinking sensation I felt every day when my neighbor's mother dropped me off at home—and the evening my anxieties proved all too justified. Drunk as usual, my father had chosen that night to voice one of his periodic conspiracy theories about my mom's supposed infidelities. Only this time, he punctuated his tirade by waving a revolver we had never seen before.

- Some people aspire to a law degree apparently from birth; others back into it after a life spent chasing other dreams. I can't say which approach is better, but for most of my life, I chased the dream of becoming a world-champion surfer. Strange as it may sound, I can think of no better preparation for the law.

- November 14, 2004. As I was introduced as P&G Munich's new sales liaison, I looked around and saw the same thing in every face—cold fear. Were these the same employees who just seven months earlier were celebrating a 300 percent year-over-year sales increase? Just the day before, however, P&G had dismissed 33 of their colleagues. And here was I, sent from the States by the very same ax-wielding company. "I'm excited to be in Germany; I love your beer" just wasn't going to cut it.

- "The best of both worlds." That phrase precisely captures the gratifying double life of legal practice and technological exploration I live every day as a patent examiner for the U.S. Patent and Trade Office—the largest institutional defender of intellectual property in the world. For the past two years, I have immersed myself in the pleasurable duty of evaluating the scope, validity, and originality of inventions produced by some of the planet's brightest minds. On my analysis, recommendation, and knowledge of the law hinges the decision to award 20-year monopolies to ideas that can make—or break—entire corporations.

- "What's it like being the daughter of the Secretary of State?" the journalist asked, thrusting his microphone in my face. I smiled my "famous person's child" smile, which long ago became practiced at hiding the enormity of the challenge my father's brilliance and success have always posed for me.

- "Where did we go wrong?" The disappointment in my dissertation advisor's voice when I told him I was going to law school was unmistakable. "You're going to have a great academic career; why throw it away?"

- On May 28, 2000, my life was changed forever when I swerved to avoid a metal frame hurtling toward me and sent my Harley careering down a ravine at 60 miles an hour. The next thing I knew a doctor was telling me I had broken my neck at the C–5 level and would never walk again.

- Hubris comes in all shapes and sizes. It has even been known to take the form of a college freshman named Davis Corcoran. If you had asked, I would have described myself as a modest, even self-effacing soul. That is not apparently how my classmates viewed me as I raised my hand to respond to Professor Janssen's comment about the Stars and Bars flying over South Carolina's statehouse.

- When I was 10, I accepted a dare from a friend and consumed 228 M&M's in the space of nine and a half minutes. I still can't say which punishment was worse: my parents' scolding or my violent bellyache.

- You can find the origin of my journey to law school right there in section 243.9 of the California penal code. When I first came across the entry for "Battery by Gassing" I imagined some strange offense involving automobile fuel or perhaps homicidal neo-Nazis. But the reality was just as bizarre—and fascinating. "Battery by gassing" refers to prison convicts "intentionally placing or throwing . . . any human excrement or other bodily fluids or bodily substances" at detention facility peace officers. It was the charge against Van Nguyen, a tattooed and surly Ventura County gang member, and it was my job to reduce that strange offense to a misdemeanor.

- As we crested the white-capped winter waves south of New Zealand, Eric and I suddenly came upon a massive, steel-gray whaling ship—a "sushi factory on steroids," he called it—anchored stolidly in the icy waters. "That's the *Tochigi Maru*," Eric exclaimed with a mixture of fear and disgust.

- The glass splintered on impact. I felt more than heard the dull thud of Tom's fist against the frigid windshield. It was my senior year of high school. Sitting in Tom's Mustang, we had gotten into another silly argument when, before I realized what was happening, he became incensed and slammed his fist into the windshield. For over a year, I had endured his insults, threats, physical abuse, and manipulation, but as I willed myself to look from the fractured glass to Tom's bloodied hand, I realized for the first time the depth of violence that lay beneath his attractive exterior. At that moment I stepped out of his car and his life for the last time.

■ Because preconceived assumptions have never applied to me, I know they can't be applied to others. As the youngest in a family that claims equal parts Inuit, Italian, Senegalese, and Chinese roots, I learned early to appreciate my differences and, by extension, to be sensitive to them in others.

■ "We really need a man for that position." Though at first I could not believe my ears, those eight words banished forever my naive belief that discrimination could not exist at Beecham Industries.

■ Leaving for work the morning of June 2, 2006, the last outcome I would have guessed awaited me was the loss of all my worldly possessions save the ones I was driving and wearing. Three and a half hours later, the aging furnace in my 80-year-old apartment erupted into a three-alarm blaze, incinerating my valuables, family photos, cat, and nearly concluded dissertation.

- Twenty years ago, a young man seeking to do good walked into a boy's life and through his generosity and kindness changed it forever. I am that boy, and if it were not for the guidance and mentorship of that man, Kijana Mbeki, I would not be here today. I was seven years old when my mother decided to enroll me in the Lehigh Valley Big Brother program that would give me the positive male role model I had lacked since my parents' divorce.

- By living, working, or traveling in over 28 cities in 11 countries, I have learned what Lou Holtz meant when he said, "If you want to succeed, be uncomfortable." My willingness to be vulnerable to transformation has given me multicultural skills, treasured friendships, and rich memories that have prepared me for a career in international law.

Chapter 3 Perfect Phrases for Autobiographical Personal Statements

"The personal statement should tell your 'story.'"

(Arizona)

"What circumstances, events, individuals, or institutions have influenced you and how?"

(Notre Dame)

"Describe an experience that has impacted your life or describe a person you admire."

(Alabama)

Sometimes your strongest stories will be the ones that capture your life story or the crucial defining moments or influences that have shaped you. Don't try to tell your autobiography, but communicate the essential context and key experiences that only you can tell. Autobiographical essays may use multiple incidents or details to convey the broad trajectory of your family history and your life, or they may explore one or more significant experiences in great detail. Sometimes focusing part of your personal statement on someone else—a mentor, friend, or hero—can reveal as much about you as about the person who influenced you. Whichever strategy you use, autobiographical essays must be personally revealing, honestly written, and convey not only the relevant "facts" but how you feel about them. Let's look at some perfect phrases for autobiographical essays.

Family and Upbringing

■ In junior high school I lived in morbid fear that my academic successes would pigeonhole me as a humorless nerd. Fortunately, my self-appointed role as "the game master" after school earned me a reputation as an inventive class leader. I designed and organized complex medieval or espionage role-playing games in which I served as screenwriter, director, and producer. My first real outdoor game was a medieval adventure in which 40 classmates and friends overcame various tests, traps, and hostile "creatures" to find a treasure (a wad of McDonald's gift coupons) hidden in the woods outside Hanover. This admittedly weird hobby did not make me popular with girls or athletes, but it greatly developed my creativity and leadership abilities. As the game master, I was creating stories and managing the players, using negotiation and inspiration to guide my peers through complex and sometimes difficult interactions. In one particularly dicey moment, I even had to convince the local police to let us off the hook when they mistook our plastic dart pistols for real guns!

- I have the autobiographical hallmarks, I'll admit, of an aspiring lawyer. My father is a member of the bar and has practiced in three jurisdictions, rising from a prosecutor to brigadier general of the U.S. Army Judge Advocate Generals Corps (retired), the highest rank for a reserve officer. Though he never pressured me toward a law career, he was always unabashed about cultivating in me a lawyer's communication skills. When I prepared for a class presentation in third grade, he watched and made suggestions on my presence and style, including how to use emphatic hand gestures with courtroom effectiveness. These skills served me well when I became president of my high school class as a sophomore and then president of my school's forensics team. Volunteering in Congressman Daltrey's office just across from my school deepened my interest in the law and my profile as a likely "prelaw" candidate. I nevertheless arrived at my summer internship at the Supreme Court deeply unsure that the law could ever be my calling.

- The childhood memories I cherish most are the summer vacations we spent with our grandparents at their country farmhouse near Madrid. My grandfather, now 86, was a fanatical supporter of Francisco Franco, and after getting howling drunk, he would excoriate the "republicanos" with such bitter contempt that even I, a political innocent, trembled. Yet despite those nightly rants, our summer holidays with Grampa Federico were idylls. My sister, brothers, and I spent entire days wandering happily among the vineyards, climbing trees, and chasing goats. It was my first exposure to the truth that love and hatred, the dark and the light, can go hand in hand.

- Eating a hard-boiled egg at the summit of Mount Fuji requires a daring palate and the good sense to pinch your nose ever so lightly, to avoid being overwhelmed by the sulfuric odor from the area's indigenous hot springs. This odoriferous treat was my parents' idea of a reward for my not complaining during our seven-hour ascent to the revered volcano's crater. At 10, I was too young to appreciate the significance of our trip up the honored "Fuji-San." Indeed, the lasting object of my attention was my father's hiking stick, which was branded with a dozen indecipherable kanji indicating the waypoints along our route. That walking stick, which I still possess and can now read fluently, remains a metaphor for my lifelong journey to embrace new cultures, new languages, and new challenges.

- My intense curiosity about the world stems directly from my childhood. Growing up in an isolated valley of the Ch'ang-pai Mountains, I had a burning desire— unsatisfied until I was eight—to see what was on the other side of the summits surrounding our home. My father, a tax collector, was the first in his family to attend college, and he raised me to understand the value of education and self-reliance. In 1998, my family and I immigrated to the United States, but when my grandfather fell terminally ill a year later, my parents returned to China to care for him. I was only 17, but I made a gut decision to stay in the United States and fend for myself, against my parents' direct wishes. As a child of a culture in which obeying one's elders is bred in the bone, it took everything I had to disobey my parents. I was on my own.

- I used to pray my friends wouldn't see my father's dirty hands. I feared that as soon as they saw those nails permanently blackened with dirt and blueberry stains and those fingers cracked from snapping off rose thorns, I would incur some fatal social judgment and be banished from polite society. Today, I cherish those hands as symbols of my father's dedication to his father's fruit market, now Portland's only remaining local grocery chain. I was never embarrassed by my mother's hands or those of her family, which were the giving hands of doctors, nurses, social workers, a nun, and teachers. In perpetual motion creating a loving, Christian home for our family of eight (including two foster children), my mother's hands joined my father's to lift me into an adulthood dedicated to the same values of hard work and concern that guide me to law school today.

Key Experiences

■ It was two months into my junior year of high school, and my friend Alex and I were dropping my date off at her house after a Halloween party. Her neighbors, who were hosting a noisy party for what I immediately recognized was a local gang, identified us as hailing from their rival gang's neighborhood. "Hey, you know you can't come here!" one shouted, throwing a menacing glance and then a beer can in our direction. Moments later, two of the neighbors exited the yard and came toward us, and Alex immediately broke into a dead sprint toward his car. Without a look back, he sped off, knocking one of the gang members down on his way. As I looked back in disbelief, I saw one gang member holding a handgun. Obviously high, he shouted something indecipherable at me as I began a mad dash toward home. I could almost feel the bullets clipping the pavement around me as I flew down the sidewalk and through several backyards. I spent the next three hours under a car, praying, crying, and wondering what would happen next.

- "I'm sorry, but my dad said I can't kiss you because you're a Mormon." I had heard stories about anti-Mormon prejudice, but I had managed to make it to junior high school before I was directly wounded by someone else's intolerance. It was the eighth-grade prom and, Jennifer Lee, the cutest girl in class, was my date. For a blissful moment it no longer mattered that I was only a thin and gawky nonathlete; with Jennifer at my side I was the big man on campus. We had had a fun evening, but as I leaned closer to end my triumph with an innocent goodnight kiss, Jennifer pulled sharply away. I was embarrassed, of course, but nothing she had said or done all evening prepared me for the 14 words she uttered next. Perhaps in reaction to my shock, she abruptly ran into her house and slammed the door behind her. As I walked, dazed, down Jennifer's front walk back to my parents' car, the world seemed a harshly different place.

- The day I gave up my dream of a music career felt like the end of my life. Practicing four hours a day from age six, I had become skilled enough by high school to win three regional performance awards, a teen violin competition in San Francisco, and—my proudest moment—a full-tuition scholarship to study at the Nashville Conservatory under the retired virtuoso Klaus Delfs. Fed by dreams of solo-career glory, by my sophomore year I was sustaining a regular concert and recital schedule that took me across the country, and I had begun teaching teenage students. In my junior year, I learned of an opportunity to become a pupil of Itzhak Ruggieri at the legendary Curtis Institute. After weeks of constant practice, I played for him in his private studio off Locust Street for an entire morning. His comments were positive, even kind, but the thrust of his judgment was unmistakable: a career as a concert violinist was not an option for me. Though I transferred to the Curtis Institute that year, my playing was never the same. The challenging pieces I had tackled with gusto before, now took me longer to master, practicing became less endurable, and the delight I had previously taken in praise was diminished. When I finished a distant sixth in the Los Angeles Chamber Musicians competition my senior year, I knew my first life was over.

- We'd been warned to leave town early, but even 5 a.m. wasn't early enough. The gathering mob had beaten us to the station and was making sure that no buses got out. My friends and I, all Shiites from southwest Baghdad, were visiting Fallujah during a military training trip when we suddenly became targets as Sunnis began full-scale rioting against the imposition of Shiite control. Racing the mob to another bus stop outside town, we watched the (fortunately empty) bus ahead of us endure heavy stoning before being overturned and set afire. I knew our lives depended entirely on what kind of person our bus's driver turned out to be. What tribe claimed his allegiance? What was the likelihood that after five years of war he had enough humanity and courage left to stay with us and drive us through the mob?

■ Shanice, a 17-year-old high school senior, was my patient when she suffered, through no identifiable human error, an extremely rare brain injury during a routine appendectomy. This unusual complication—its etiology remains unexplained—left her completely paralyzed. Her hearing, vision, and sense of touch were fine, but she could not blink, talk, walk, or move any muscle voluntarily. Every day, virtually her entire high school came to Roosevelt Memorial's ICU to see Shanice. I too saw her daily, held her hand, spoke to her and her friends and family. It was heart-rending beyond words to see her lying still in her bed when shortly before she had been laughing and joking with the

➡

nurses and her baby brother, Trevon. During Shanice's stay in the ICU, I came home every night emotionally exhausted and alternately depressed and angry that such an inexplicable calamity could have occurred to so healthy and vivacious a girl. I tried to seek solace in colleagues' support and such platitudes as "everything happens for a reason," but they didn't work. After six weeks Shanice developed pneumonia and passed away. I had endured patients' deaths before and even prided myself on my ability to cordon off the emotions that every doctor confronts when treating patients whose personalities, hopes, and pains are so vividly on display. Shanice's death made me question whether I was cut out for a medical career.

- The impact of moving to Manhattan from Djakarta for college was both subtle and total. Although my values are the same, I now have a much deeper confidence in my instincts. I know I can adapt to new challenges and learn unfamiliar topics quickly. And though living overseas has given me a greater appreciation for being American, I now see myself as a "permanent" citizen of the most mysterious and exciting city in the world.

- It was only 10 days into basic training when our drill sergeant told us to retrieve our enlistment contracts from our wall lockers. We sat on the polished tiles and read for the first time the clause that says you can be reassigned "in time of war." Sergeant Olson then turned on the television, and grimly we watched scenes of warfare in Afghanistan. We had been reassigned to infantry training. Next stop: Operation Enduring Freedom. Surviving boot camp at Camp Lejeune became my rite of passage, a journey into the deepest part of me. Ultimately, I overcame my fears and doubts and guided a squad of men shaken by suicides and an unforeseen war into becoming more than they had known how to be before. I began my defining moment as a 19-year-old boy surrounded by strangers. I emerged from it leading men who had become my brothers.

Key Influences

- Was I descended from a traitor or a hero? Only by discovering the truth about my great grandfather—perhaps hidden here in my family's old home in Dordogne—could I find the answer. After Germany's invasion of France in 1940, German "businessmen" roamed France demanding war booty. As the descendant of a long line of antique dealers, Mathieu Allègre, my maternal great grandfather, faced this choice: surrender family treasures or somehow trick the Germans. Removing the unprinted end sheets from ninth-century agricultural reports, Allègre painstakingly printed an exacting replica of *Les Serments de Strassbourg* and convinced the Germans that this was the priceless original agreement signed in 842 by two of Charlemagne's grandsons. By doing so, Allègre saved our family's collection of very real treasures and used the proceeds to found Dordogne's now world-famous antique dealership, L'Chevalier Connoisseur Society. I was descended from a genuine hero. That was our family's story anyway. The document Allègre sold the Germans was destroyed in the war; only photographs of it survive today. But studying these photos, some French and German experts have claimed that my great grandfather actually sold one of only two surviving copies of *Les Serments de Strassbourg*. If they are right, Allègre had committed treason. As I explored every cubbyhole and crevice of the family's ancestral home, the mystery of Mathieu Allègre grew.

- "Let's go see Mrs. Jenns," was Dr. Brian Melman's way of recruiting me for an after-hours house call late last year. It was 9 p.m., and we had already been on call for two days. I knew he couldn't have slept more than a few hours because I had been with him. Though 30 years my senior, he looked ready to climb Mount Everest—or pay a house call on a dying patient. Dr. Melman inspires me with his intelligence and clinical expertise but also with his indefatigable attitude. For him, pharmacology, physiology, biochemistry, all the scientific aspects of medicine, are just gateways to the more rewarding subject: helping sick people. About to start my third consecutive night on call, I asked him how he maintains his energy and enthusiasm. "It's easy. As bad as I sometimes feel, and sometimes that's pretty rotten, I know that what the patient is going through is much worse."

- My brother Jason was my friend, my first mentor, and my toughest competitor. When he became our state's high school wrestling champion in 2000, I practiced with and learned from him until in 2001 I took the title from him. When he handed me the tournament cup at the awards ceremony, he gave me his "keep tryin', little brother—it won't help" smile and whispered in my ear: "You'll be giving this back to me next year." I excelled in sports, school, and life because of the determination and leadership I learned from Jason. Telling me, "I want to serve my country," he become a Special Forces volunteer in Iraq in 2003. Although a sniper's bullet took him from me 18 months ago, he'll always be the person I look up to most.

- Even today, the people of Brockton, Ohio, still debate how my grandfather survived. Five years ago, crossing the street in the farming town he rarely left, my 78-year-old grandfather was struck by a speeding car and lay in the deserted road for almost an hour before a neighbor found him. He lost his leg in the accident, but amazingly never voiced any anger or desire for vengeance. "The driver probably didn't see me," he charitably offers, and regrets only that running his farm is harder now. When relatives advised my grandfather to sell his farm and move to Columbus where we could look after him, he protested that that would be like losing his other leg, and he never let us raise the subject again. After the operation he bought farm equipment that he could operate with one leg and continued running his organic farm with the same tirelessness as before. Everything takes him longer now, but even at age 83 his farm is productive, and he remains the simple, cheerful man he always was. I thought a lot about my grandfather as I contemplated leaving my father's dairy business for law school. He was the only member of my family to encourage my career switch, though he could easily have chosen to view it as a rejection of the vocation he's devoted his life to.

■ If my mother's influence explains my passion for words, it is because of my father that I'm a chronic tinkerer. His inventive puttering with things electronic and mechanical and his fascination with astronomy inspired him to build an eight-inch reflector telescope literally from scratch when I was in grade school. Growing up, whenever I got my hands on something I would, like him, disassemble and examine it, attempt to improve it, and occasionally successfully reassemble it. In the eighth grade, I built a large contraption with nine motor-actuated slide projectors (which I also built from scratch) that sat above a diorama of the World War I battlefield at Reims. The projectors cast moving photographs of German and French troops on the diorama to stage a reenactment of the Second Battle of the Marne. In the years since then, I have also disassembled and rebuilt a 1952 Jaguar XK120, a 1947 Piper Cub, and an early Weather Bureau satellite. When I told my parents I planned a career in patent law, my father and mother just smiled at each other as though they'd won a bet.

Chapter 4 Perfect Phrases for Challenges and Disadvantages

"Applicants have, for example, elaborated on . . . significant obstacles met and overcome; . . . socioeconomic challenges; . . . or experiences and perspectives relating to disadvantage, disability, or discrimination."

(Michigan)

"If applicable, you may also describe any disadvantages that may have adversely affected your past performance or that you have successfully overcome, including linguistic barriers or a personal or family history of cultural, educational or socioeconomic disadvantage."

(University of California Berkeley)

L aw schools believe that they can find out a lot about how applicants will deal with the challenge of a law career by seeing how they've dealt with the challenges they've encountered already. Applicants who have come through a lot to get where they are today will be viewed with special favor by admissions readers who are happy to reward determination and focus. Making difficult decisions, overcoming obstacles, battling through resistance—all of these can make powerful material for challenge-type essays. Let's look at some challenge and disadvantage perfect phrases.

> ■ My father was born in the wilds of northern Wyoming, but after earning a scholarship to Yale and then a J.D. at Harvard Law, he settled in Manhattan, where he met and eventually married my mother. After I finished fourth grade, my parents decided to spend a year in Paris, and they sent me to live with my grandparents in the small Wyoming ranching town of Rail Gap. Even at my resilient young age the lifestyle contrasts between Rail Gap and Manhattan's Upper East Side were a major shock. Instead of the personal maid who had prepared my choice of breakfasts on East 89th Street, I had to quickly develop culinary self-sufficiency when my grandparents told me the only "vittles" were biscuits n' cream gravy. Instead of a five-minute limousine ride to The Brearley School, I found myself thrown into the Wyoming winter cold every morning for a bumpy 45-minute bus ride to Rail Gap Elementary, a place that perfectly conformed to my mental image of a penitentiary for the criminally insane.
>
> ➡

- That inspiring success story was dealt a serious blow when I developed anorexia at age 14. After struggling for two years with this debilitating eating disorder, I was admitted to a hospital program the summer before my sophomore year. At St. Luke's, I met girls like me who were so malnourished they had to limit how much they walked to minimize the calories they burned. Other girls hadn't successfully kept a meal down for many months. The St. Luke's program taught us how to gain weight and meet our nutritional needs, but it also gave me my first lesson in how inadequately the American health-care system treats mental illness. I won't forget my anger when I first learned that girls I had grown to care about were forced to leave our $1,250-a-day program despite dangerously low blood pressure, osteoporosis, or irregular heartbeat—all because their inpatient treatment insurance coverage was limited or had expired.

- When my father moved our family from Egypt to the United States in 1990, he sacrificed a solid career, a comfortable lifestyle, and a respected role in Cairo's academic community so my sister and I could receive American educations. Despite his Ph.D. and extensive curriculum vitae, he struggled in the United States, working as an assistant professor at a community college for five years before trying to strike out on his own as a consulting engineer—with mixed results. When I asked him once why he had made all these sacrifices, he said only that we were not only his children but his duty. I lost my chance to fully thank him for this gift when he unexpectedly died of a heart attack in 1997, a week before his forty-seventh birthday. My father's legacy of integrity, determination, and selflessness kept me going as I, though only 12, tried to be the "man in the family" for my devastated mother.

■ The lesson that you can't always get what you want is one I learned early in life. As the son of a United flight attendant, I grew up around airplanes and airports, sparking my boyhood dream to become a fighter pilot. I was heartbroken to learn that my nearsightedness disqualified me from the military's pilot training programs. My parents' disclosure that they couldn't afford private flying lessons deepened my disappointment. There are some challenges, it seems, that you just can't overcome. At age 16 I filed my flying dreams away and focused on goals I could achieve. It wasn't until my second year as a junior engineer at IBM that I realized I could now afford the flying lessons I'd given up on eight years before.

■ "If you don't reach a compromise in 15 minutes, consider your bill dead." The Civic Affairs Committee chairman's warning to me inspired a chorus of moans from the rest of the committee, as their visions of a quick end-of-session flight home for the holidays quickly faded. I knew better than to butt heads with a state senator who was late for a plane and peeved at a late-adjourning committee meeting. But as Senator Raj Daniwal's legislative aide it was my job in his absence to present his bill to fund new security equipment for the state police—and to defend it against Senator Lawson's attempts to attach completely untenable amendments for the express purpose of dooming our bill to failure. Visualizing Senator Daniwal's reaction when I told him I had let his "slam-dunk" bill die in committee, I summoned my courage and strode to the podium. "Mr. Chairman, " I said, sure everyone had heard my voice crack with anxiety, "I would respectfully ask for the committee's indulgence for 15 minutes as I try to resolve this issue with the chairman's good friend." In the next quarter hour I learned more about compromise, negotiation, and diplomacy than I had ever imagined there was to know. Channeling my desperation into creativity, I offered six language modifications that eliminated Senator Lawson's opposition but preserved Senator Lawson's funding, and the bill passed out of committee intact. An hour later I was boarding my plane to Chicago.

■ "Oh my god, you were placed at Cherry Street!" My teacher-in-training classmates at Concordia University consoled me as word spread that my first trial-by-fire as a public school teacher would occur in one of the Twin Cities' least "comfortable and convenient" schools— Cherry Street High School in St. Paul's tough inner city. Soon I learned some of the grim details about Cherry Street: a school administrator had been gunned down when his shady business dealings went awry; a child of one of the teachers assaulted someone with a deadly weapon, and so on. I can't say I was surprised then when on my first day in class my students challenged me directly, complaining, "Why do we have to learn this?" Seeing that at Cherry Street respect had to be earned, I began telling them my story. As a high school student, I had hated studying and much preferred the basketball court, until a teacher who knew my family informed me that if I scored well enough on the SAT, I could earn scholarships to college—enabling my mother to quit one of the two jobs she was working to fund my education. By overcoming my fear of mathematics, I earned a high enough score to win a tuition-free ride at the University of Wisconsin. When my Cherry Street students realized my background was no different from theirs, they began to see me as a role model for their own success. It's true that I had to send the occasional student to detention, but most gradually showed motivation to learn. Two months later, when

I stayed late to help the students prepare for the SAT, the entire class showed up.

- My parents were divorced when I was only nine, and I haven't seen my dad in over 15 years. I'm told he's an addicted gambler. After he left, my mom had to work two jobs to make ends meet. My brother Vertis and I grew up as latchkey kids, and I started working at my uncle's restaurant when I was just 13. Despite the challenges, my mother, brother, and I found ways to enjoy life, and growing up in a one-parent household with an absent, unsuccessful father helped make me capable, resourceful, and compassionate. It will also make me a capable, resourceful, and compassionate lawyer. Each potential client will have individual circumstances for seeking my counsel. Understanding clients and their problems will be as important as understanding the law.

- After a preliminary analysis, I decided to commit my life savings of $150,000 to founding a company to build the apartment building, since I lacked the resources to develop it myself. All I needed was the owner's commitment to invest $1.5 million! I did a meticulous feasibility analysis, which demonstrated that the development would realize the owner a 55 percent return. I made a thorough presentation to the owner, underscoring the higher profit potential of an apartment building, recommending a reputable architect, and assuring him that my company would be staffed with industry veterans. When he still held back, I threw in a $2,000 daily late penalty. After I assembled my team, work began.

■ My wife Dawn had had morning sickness before, but this was something different. Early into her pregnancy, Dawn's symptoms worsened, so I had her move back to Atlanta where her parents could take better care of her and our two-year-old daughter, Aimee. When Dawn began repeatedly vomiting blood, however, I took an advance leave and immediately returned to Georgia. The test results showed high levels of thyroid hormones—harmless if caused by pregnancy, but, if they were preexisting, they could potentially affect both Dawn and our baby. I immediately requested a leave of absence from my analyst's position and stayed by Dawn's hospital bed until she and the baby were fine. I was shocked to learn on my return three weeks later that all my work had been reassigned to another analyst. The manager I had willingly sacrificed evenings and weekends for for two years muttered something about "needing people I can count on" and indicated vaguely that the promotion he had promised had "encountered some resistance." Two months later I was let go—downsized. Though I was

➡

devastated, Dawn's illness had reminded me of what I really care about. We are resolved to love and care for our new child, normal or not, and our lives will probably never be the same. I know now that I will succeed in transitioning into the law, but I also know what I didn't before—that my most important consideration now will always be the needs and wishes of my family. They will always come first.

- As union workers, Ford's line workers do not live in fear of their managers. Hence, supervisors who do not know the union rules, are too autocratic, or just rub workers the wrong way are given a form of union hazing that has ruined management careers. I knew at the outset of my six-day test in October 2005 that as an Asian female college graduate I was starting off different from the typical line worker in at least three ways. If I failed to mesh with them, I could potentially be held back professionally, and my hopes of being invited into Ford's Young Manager Training program for high-potential managers would be dashed.

- I asked doctors in the unit how they could deal with such intense, emotionally wrenching moments. Several replied that they detached themselves emotionally; others said that it was just "part of the job." But I was uncomfortable with the idea of diminishing the sensitivity to human suffering that had motivated me to practice medicine in the first place. Pressing ahead with my clinical exposure as a volunteer in Portland University Medical Center's critical care unit, I experienced other heart-rending moments with distraught and grieving parents and spouses. Discussing the problems I was having dealing with patients' death and suffering with a premed advisor, Dr. Wu, I gradually came to accept that I did not possess the unique attitude toward human suffering that is required of surgeons and critical care doctors.

- I was a sophomore in high school when my father decided to take a job in Texas. My brother and I were to stay in Florida with our mother to finish our schooling and then join him in San Antonio in the new house he planned to buy there. He did buy that house, moving all our furniture there, while we continued to live in a small furnished one-bedroom apartment near the projects. But the original one-year separation expanded into two years and then two and a half. When my father finally told us we could pack up for Texas, I was beginning college in Tallahassee and decided against transferring. Incensed, my father informed me that I could pay for my college education on my own—beginning with next quarter's tuition check! Two years later, I was making slow progress toward my degree while balancing a 35-hour workweek, when my mother called to say that my father had "fallen in love" and wanted a divorce. My mother's tone of voice, one I'd never heard before, told me it was time for me to fly to Texas and help her and my brother cope. College would have to wait.

Chapter 5 Perfect Phrases for Values and Beliefs

"What are your core values?"

(Notre Dame)

"Why do you believe you are prepared for the ethical, intellectual and time demands of law school and the legal profession?"

(North Carolina)

Another kind of personal statement helps you stand out by showing that you have the kinds of values that effective, ethical lawyers need and that the law values. Asserting your integrity, honesty, compassion, or sense of justice is far less compelling than revealing these things through a story, often one in which your ethics are directly tested. Let's look at some perfect phrases for value and belief essays.

■ "Can you get me outta here? I know they're tryin' to kill me." My image of what a summer internship with Maine's Attorney General's office might entail did not, I'll admit, include fielding phone calls from desperate and probably delusional inmates at state medical care facilities. To be honest, I had pictured the state's AG office as a bureaucratic sinecure, a quiet, slow-moving place where documents were methodically moved from one stack to another but where nothing substantive ever happened. As the founder and president of my high school's Conservative Club, I took it as an article of faith that bureaucrats were an ineffectual, time-serving bunch. As soon as I arrived in the office's Medicaid fraud division, however, I realized how wrong I had been. To support the office's efforts to investigate and prosecute cases of physician fraud, patient abuse, or patient neglect by care facility workers, I searched for (and not infrequently found) evidence that dentists had overbilled their patients and summarized reports of abuse incidents. These time-consuming assignments could be monotonous, but they introduced me to the critical behind-the-scenes spadework that goes into helping attorneys assemble a litigable case. But it was the anguished phone calls I sometimes fielded from patients claiming abuse that taught me the most. Though their complaints often sounded more imagined than real, I was startled by their stories of brazen neglect and mistreatment and moved by their desperation and pain. I was also frustrated by how little I or my office mates could do to help them, and I found myself wishing that the AG's office had greater latitude to investigate and prosecute their claims. Though my three-month stint working side by side with government bureaucrats did not change my belief that big government is often inefficient and wasteful, it forever cured me of my contempt for bureaucrats and the instincts that motivate them to serve.

■ All my personal values are reflected in my commitment to becoming a minister for the New Light Family Church. The church's ministry program shows individuals how to develop sound ministries by offering coursework in everything from communication and church administration to biblical history. On graduating from the two-year program, many students seek work as full- or part-time ministers in one of New Light's churches. After months of New Light's 35-hour school weeks (including homework)—on top of my full-time position at Boeing that required me to rise at 4 a.m— I was proud to graduate from the ministry program with a 4.0 grade point average. Aside from giving me the chance to channel my faith into a part-time career of service to others, the ministry program enabled me to form bonds with people I deeply admire—my fellow ministers.

■ As young as I was, I understood that going to school was the only opportunity I would have to break out of the smothering environment of Shuwayhitiyah, where girls had no choice but to listen to their parents or husbands all their lives. I wanted independence. I wanted freedom—freedom from poverty, freedom from a sexist system, freedom from a system where parents decided everything. This burning desire for freedom has remained the most important theme of my life and will always be what drives me.

■ Living and working both in the United States and in Brazil has enabled me to see through and help tear down the stereotypes prevalent in both countries. I have been shocked to hear well-educated Americans ask me, "Does Brazil have paved roads?" or, "How many people in the world speak Brazilian?" And instead of surrendering to the nationalistic mentality that requires everyone in Brazil to criticize America, I tell my Brazilian friends about the Americans I have met who speak their language, know their history and culture, and have done more traveling across Brazil than the majority of Brazilians. The lesson that splitting my life equally between both countries has taught me is one that

I wish were obvious to everyone: yes, people are different in race, religion, and the like, but at the end of the day people are people. We all have the same ambitions, needs, and fears.

■ Only in 1975, with the Family Reform Law, had traditional Italy granted women equal legal status. Before then—within my own lifetime—the *codice civile* stated that "the wife shall follow the civil conditions that [the husband] provides . . . she is obliged to accompany him wherever he sees fit." The reformed civil code made husbands and wives equal legal entities in the marriage, but only on paper. From personal experience, I can attest that women are still routinely asked in job interviews if they are engaged, married, or plan to have children. As recently as 2001, the Court of Cassation (Italy's supreme court) ruled that a husband had grounds for divorce if his wife did not "satisfactorily" do the household chores. A 1999 decision even bordered on the absurd when it stated that a woman couldn't be raped if she was wearing jeans because, "It is common experience that it is almost impossible to take a pair of jeans off another person without his or her help since it is already difficult enough [to take them off] for the person who is wearing them." Since the woman had taken off her jeans, she had consented.

- In high school, my English teacher counseled us all to strive to be "Renaissance men." The ideal of the well-rounded citizen-leader struck a deep chord in me, and in the years since I have tried to live an eclectic life of creativity, public service, leadership, and intellectual accomplishment. At the University of Washington, for example, I joined Amnesty International as a research officer and learned the importance of careful research and intellectual rigor. My work in traditional Spanish dance and my 10 years of formal music study developed my creative faculties, and as a sometime professional pianist I have performed with the Dallas Youth Symphony, the Seattle Kamerata, and the Santa Barbara Mozarteum. Similarly, as an organizer for Pink Jeep Tours of Arizona I honed my leadership skills organizing outdoor adventures in Sedona, from hot-air balloon trips to horseback trail rides. Closer to my professional life, I have worked as a lab assistant at the University of Washington's department of oncology and a researcher in its department of radiology.

- The role Kristine described sounded great until she told me the client would be informed I was an "expert" in ATM systems. I had a good technology background, but not in the electronic funds industry or its transaction systems. Deciding I could not justify misrepresenting my background and capability, I declined the ATM project three days after Kristine's offer. She asked me to rethink my decision, but I was firm.

- The past few months have been pivotal for Taiwan's gay community. Late last fall, a gay man convicted of murder in Taipei was given an unusually harsh sentence simply because he was gay. I spent three weeks participating in the Gay Rights Coalition's effort to find scientific evidence refuting the prosecutor's argument that gay people are by nature "threateningly aggressive." Fortunately, in the face of our opposition the prosecutor revoked his position at the last minute. But just two months later, Taiwan's only gay magazine was harassed by a government agency because it "corrupts the moral fiber of the society." Moreover, more and more gay people in Taiwan have been falling victim to blackmailing and gay bashing because our demands for the inclusion of a sexual orientation clause in the National Human Rights Law are being ignored. In the face of these developments, I've had to ask myself whether my values as a human being and as a gay man are something I can afford to defend on merely a part-time basis. I've concluded they demand my defense as a professional human rights attorney.

- As I read the project prospectus, I noticed the glaring omission of the expensive gas-scrubbing equipment OSHA requires for all U.S. tests. Clearly, Enerplex was trying to take advantage of Guatemala's weak air-quality standards. Without such gas-scrubbing equipment our Guatemalan workers would be exposed to carcinogenic toxins like benzene and dioxins. After hours of deliberation, I decided that rejecting the assignment on moral grounds would not help the Guatemalan workers who faced exposure—someone else would just take the job. I therefore informed my manager that I would accept the assignment only if he would also nominate me as the safety officer of the pilot experiment. Later, I persuaded him to allocate a modest budget for protective organic vapor masks, and while in Guatemala I trained the local workers in their use and explained the dangers of prolonged exposure.

■ My father's belief in moral clarity ensured that the educations my brothers and I received adhered firmly to Christian values and ethics, despite the sad influence of Paraguay's corrupted social culture. Since the 1980s, political parties have transformed Paraguay into the most corrupt democracy in South America, spreading unethical behavior into every level of the social and judicial systems. My country's corruption is so overwhelming that many Paraguayans just give up trying to change it. Just as lifeguards are taught to let a panicking victim drown, many sometimes feel that the best decision is simply to blend into the corruption—

"to play the game." Indeed, the common opinion on the street is that if you want to become rich and successful in Paraguay, you have to become a politician. Because my father believed that education was the only thing that could get Paraguay past such corruption, he sent all four of my brothers and me to the most expensive international school in Asunción, the American School.

■ During Pacific Northwest Trust's long attempt to acquire Nuvatrix, a major biotech firm in Silicon Valley, I worked closely with "Will," Nuvatrix's assistant treasurer, over eight months. One morning after a working session, he asked me if local newspaper reports that Pacific Northwest's takeover plan included laying off his company's employees were true. Since I hadn't seen the reports, I didn't answer him on the spot, but his question put me in a difficult situation. Pacific Northwest was in fact seriously evaluating a contingent layoff plan. On my way back to Seattle, I struggled with how to respond to Will. My personal instinct to be truthful contradicted my loyalty to Pacific Northwest's interests. Over the previous eight months, Will and I had developed a good working relationship and even friendship. By asking me whether Pacific Northwest intended to downsize Nuvatrix after our acquisition, he was clearly demonstrating his trust in me. But I also felt just as strongly that, as a Pacific

Northwest employee, I needed to guard the confidentiality of our takeover plan.

- In an instant, I knew exactly how the choices before me would play out. If I just ignored my mistake, I would get my security badge, be on my way into the vault, and begin working. There was no way they would ask me to present a U.S. passport or birth certificate. However, if I truthfully pointed out that my badge erroneously identified me as a U.S. citizen, not only would they ask to see my green card, but, worse, my own negligence would be exposed: in all my excitement about seeing Fort Knox, I had completely forgotten that I needed to bring my green card to enter a federal facility! Besides the personal embarrassment, our team would be short one auditor for at least a day, I would have to trouble a friend to mail the card down, and I'd perhaps be seen as unprofessional by Firstar's management.

- In overcoming the traumas of my childhood, I have learned how to lead from venture capital executives, CEOs like Steve Jobs and Steve Ballmer, foreign ambassadors, and church leaders. I have interacted successfully with poor Indonesian city kids, American farmers' sons, and Costa Rican migrant workers. I have caught (carefully) piranha and crocodiles in Venezuela's rivers, defended gay employees from abuse in a Wal-Mart call center, cataloged Russian Orthodox religious icons for a private collector, and taken a three-month sabbatical to travel around Sri Lanka with a Tamil student. The core value that will inform my contribution to Cornell Law is this: if my own life can change so dramatically, then I owe it to my Cornell peers to share my message of faith in personal potential; openness to others, diversity, and change; and the joyful pursuit of personal passions.

Chapter 6 Perfect Phrases for Accomplishments

"What has been your most significant accomplishment?"

(Iowa)

"You may also choose to discuss particular achievements . . . that have not already been addressed in this application."

(Boston University)

Personal statements that focus on an accomplishment give you the chance to show that you have the skills and personality to affect your environment in major ways—a key trait for law students and lawyers alike. What stories make for strong accomplishments essays? Good candidates are those experiences in which your impact was substantial and affected others positively and in which you learned something about yourself or the world. Ideally, they will be recent stories that give the reader some insights into how you deploy your strengths, whether in professional, academic, or personal environments. Here are some perfect phrases for accomplishments:

- When BCG's analysts program came to a close in May 2008, I looked for an alternative to the strict paradigm of profits and losses. Barack Obama's presidential campaign gave me that and crystallized my goal of building a career in which I could affect policy and society in a way I could be proud of. I tried for months to be actively involved. Eventually, Obama's deputy campaign director finally gave me a shot: running the motorcade for Senator Obama and his wife's private weekend in Chicago. I executed my unusual duties scrupulously—even meeting the candidate—and after my involvement in only seven other events, I was promoted to press lead, the second-highest post on an advance team. Of the 350+ advance people, only 24 were press leads. I was involved in everything from selecting sites and building local media coverage to planning the logistics for up to 160 members of the local, international, and traveling press. By Election Day, I had worked over 20 events in 13 states. The culmination was my selection, despite the availability of more experienced press leads, to do the campaign's final midnight rally in Harrisburg, Pennsylvania. Rather than the normal seven days, my advance team had 36 hours to pull the event together. We not only filled the airport hangar with 3,000 people; but we had to turn another 5,000 away. As Obama's plane slowly rolled in front of the open hangar, with thousands of supporters screaming in jubilation and cameras illuminating the night sky, I knew I had made a difference. The lasting impact of this experience was not the bright lights and media excitement; it was the skills I developed, the lessons I learned. Each week I found myself in a new part of the country working to persuade and coordinate community volunteers and leaders. Whether I was sitting with the chairman of The RainbowPUSH Coalition in Chicago or working with environmentalists at Yosemite, I had to be a strong communicator and an even stronger listener. On "game day," I used my leadership abilities to direct as many as 20 volunteers and team members in the execution of extremely detailed events. Each step the press took needed to be mapped out, every power outlet or sound feed had to be triple checked for functionality. In the end, I discovered that I have the problem-solving abilities to execute $20,000 to $100,000 events week after week without a major hitch.

■ As the truck, lurching and groaning, lowered the yellow monster to the ground, I thought to myself, "What have I gotten myself into this time?" I had rented the massive thing with only a phone call and a credit card number, so how hard could this be, right? Upon witnessing my awe at the Cat's size, the deliveryman decided that I, a 23-year-old female, probably needed a quick lesson. His lecture all-too-quickly completed, the kind deliveryman gave me a wink and a nod and left me sitting atop a shiny yellow Caterpillar backhoe loader. Leveling the playing surface of a softball field and then building a 10-foot warning track are hardly tasks to be taken lightly, let alone by a driver uninitiated in the mysteries of manual transmission. But they were unquestionably mine, because as the assistant softball coach at Dakota Regents University my duties included "ballfield maintenance," as well as recruiting, tutoring, coordinating planned giving, arranging road trips, analyzing film, and bookkeeping. After numerous attempts, I finally figured out how to drive a stick shift, how to navigate all the levers, buttons, and switches to do what I wanted to do, and how to scrape and level while in reverse (don't ask)—all with only minimal damage to the school's facility. The fact that I possess the skills to operate a bulldozer is, I admit, not grounds for admitting me as a diversity candidate, but I believe the reasons behind my bulldozing ability surely are. Let me explain.

■ The climax of the journey came in the early hours of the fifth day when, dizzy with pride and altitude sickness, I reached the top of Mount Logan, a 19,551-foot mountain in southwestern Yukon. It was truly an exhilarating moment. I had faced death, challenged my body beyond its limits, and become one of only three students who reached the summit, creating a new record for Canadian students' mountaineering. As a result, I succeeded in obtaining sponsorships worth $30,000 from companies such as Canadian Tire and Hudson's Bay Company. During my two years as president of Canadian Student Mountaineering Association, I led CSMA in summiting two other mountains higher than 5,000 meters. I also built a 120-foot-high rock wall on campus and created a rock-climbing elective with the help of classmates. Ten members of CSMA won the Royal Canadian Mountaineering Prize in 2006, and over 2,000 members joined our club during my two years at its helm. Our club received media coverage for our exploits, and students in other universities applied my approach to establish and develop their own climbing teams.

- In 2007, I finally got my chance when I joined the staff of the House Appropriations Subcommittee on Homeland Security as deputy chief of staff. As Chairman Price's appointee and close policy advisor, I initiated an ambitious schedule to create a legislative package that would make emergency supplemental appropriations available for troop readiness, veterans' care, and Hurricane Katrina recovery projects. It was a grueling process from start to finish. The nature of the legislative process ensured that each version of the bill was scrutinized endlessly by both policymakers and nonelected lobbyists, who naturally disagreed over which expenditures most deserved emergency funding and by how much. I quickly discovered that the best way to sustain momentum was to come to the table with as much knowledge as possible. In countless drafting sessions with the Office of Legislative Counsel, I learned firsthand the statutory implications of seemingly uncontroversial words like "shall" and "must." I also discovered that while sharing one's own interpretation of a statute is simple, understanding a particular statute's legal basis is not. Laws, which as a political science major I had tended to see as the product of social needs and ideology, were much more than that. One of the greatest challenges in moving the U.S. Troop Readiness, Veterans' Care, Katrina Recovery, and Iraq Accountability Appropriations Act toward passage by the House and Senate was the question of whether to raise the federal minimum wage to $7.25 per hour. If written into the bill, the increase would have set an uncomfortable precedent for the Republican members of the committee. I convinced them that they could in good conscience vote to raise the minimum wage if we could give them credit for writing in a phased-in increase: to $5.85 per hour on the sixtieth day after passage, to $6.55 per hour one year later, and to $7.25 per hour two years later. This allowed conservatives to vote for the package while still appearing to support business's interests and hold the

➡

line on government expenditures. The U.S. Troop Readiness, Veterans' Care, Katrina Recovery, and Iraq Accountability Appropriations Act was passed and signed into law on May 25, 2007. The signing ceremony at the White House remains one of the highlights of my life. I shook hands with the president, received one of the pens used to sign the bill into law, and a year later watched my brother enroll for the veterans' benefits the legislation funded.

- Because I saw the efficiencies possible through Oracle's technology, Johnson County's law firm, McKutcheon, McKutcheon & Vindaloo, gave me responsibility for leading a three-person team in engineering a data tool that can trace every investment the county entered into during the four-year period when the risky derivatives investments were made. When I completed that ahead of schedule, they asked me to create a project plan and damage analysis to explore various damage theories, which gave me the chance to work closely with high-ranking attorneys and department directors for both Johnson County and the U.S. Department of Justice. When the defendant, KMPG Investment, attempted to rebut Johnson County's damage analysis, I engineered and supervised a cash account-tracing model that showed that KMPG's insolvency claim was false—it had actually made millions during the period in question. In part because of my team's work, in June KMPG agreed to pay Johnson County $120 million in compensation for providing the poor investment advice that led to the largest municipal bankruptcy in state history. The success of the Johnson County engagement not only strengthened my company's relationship with McKutcheon, McKutcheon & Vindaloo; it also ultimately inspired me to pursue a law degree.

- In February, I helped organize HelpNow's first event, a fundraiser, in Milwaukee. I personally lined up corporate sponsorships, sold more than 50 event and raffle tickets, and hunted down potential items for the gift bag and auction. After my company, Rockwell Automation, declined to sponsor the event, I wrote a letter to the head of corporate communications and then met personally with her to persuade her that Rockwell's $5,000 donation would be benefiting an important cause. When she finally agreed, I contacted the major local banks, including Marshall & Ilsley and Associated Bank, to persuade them to donate similar amounts to the fundraiser.

- To this day, I am not sure how I moved so quickly through the ranks of YNAPAC's Washington, D.C., chapter. In only three-plus years, I went from social chair to national liaison for the local chapter. This past September, I was elected community relations director of YNAPAC's parent organization, Young Native Americans United (YNAU), a 24-chapter organization whose current membership exceeds 40,000. As the community relations director, my role is to help young Native Americans get educations and competitive jobs and increase public perception of young Native Americans as a productive force in all aspects of American life. As a member of the eight-person executive board of YNAU, I am helping the organization expand nationally, spreading the word about our 501(c)3 charitable foundation, and soliciting corporate sponsorship for our scholarship fund for college-age Native Americans.

- Working closely with Gap's business information development team to extract brand performance data, I constructed a quarterly brand performance report that included detailed analysis and performance insights. I also won support for a primary consumer target research study to address our lack of understanding of our customer. To develop a truly effective customized retail marketing program for two key retail customers, I collaborated with the sales force, media director, advertising agency, publicity team, and business information development team to develop a media plan that increased sales by 13 percent. I reinvigorated Pink Denim's isolated marketing team by building proactive relationships with other internal groups, and I gave my teammates the tools and quantitative foundation to measure their effectiveness and make the best fact-based business decisions.

- A few months after our divorce, I was awarded custody of my biological daughter, Roberta. Winning permanent custody of Chantel, my ex-wife's biological daughter, would not come so easily. Because I was not Chantel's biological father, I had no legal standing with respect to her custody. However, the juvenile courts granted me temporary custody of Chantel until her mother was able to adequately fulfill her role as a parent. Because of my tight finances, for over five years I represented myself and indirectly Chantel's interests during all the custody hearings and meetings before the Harrison County juvenile court, the Tennessee supreme court foster care review board, and Child Protective Service sessions. Throughout those long years, I prepared and responded to dozens of motions, petitions, and subpoenas, becoming, by necessity, an amateur expert in the nuances of Tennessee family law. Finally, in 2006, after five years of legal proceedings, I was awarded permanent guardianship of Chantel under a newly enacted custody law.

- To convince the dean that a new strategy was essential, I helped coordinate an electronic brainstorming session to which I invited former admissions officers, active alumni, former student admissions assistants, and professors who had reviewed applications for the admissions committee in the past. As the moderator, I got the group to identify the key challenges facing the graduate school's admissions process and to debate needed modifications. After the meeting, I summarized the group's observations, developed a new strategy for improving marketing reach and increasing yield, and vetted it with each of the participants. By creating an environment in which admissions challenges could be discussed in a nonthreatening and collaborative way, I was able to convince the dean to approve all six of my recommendations with only minor changes.

- I gained my first practical experience in tax law through a clerkship at the general counsel's office at the Baltimore Transit Authority. There, I was exposed to the tax aspects of employment benefits while helping to plan BTA's retirement and pension system. But my most exciting tax law experience was being given the chance to draft motions and analyze the Maryland state government's procurement, sales, and use-tax codes during BTA's suit against the Maryland Revenue Office and the Board of Equalization. When we won the case, I was as thrilled as our lead litigator!

- I first began to explore the role of shareholder activist about three years ago, after reviewing the sad performance of a bank-holding company in rural Cherokee County, Oklahoma, that some family members and I had invested in. My careful examination of the company's SEC filings revealed efficiency and capitalization far below that of local competitors and a loan loss reserve that, curiously, always declined despite rising loans on accrual—an old cookie jar not yet depleted. Selling out at book value seemed the wrong response, however. I knew that the law offered me another option through the privileges it extends to minority shareholders, which I decided to experiment with. When the holding company's management rejected my request for a list of shareholders, though we were clearly entitled to it under both Oklahoma statute and case law, I had no choice but to file suit in Common Pleas and, at considerable expense to the bank, negotiate the release of the list through the largest law firm in Southwest Oklahoma. We succeeded, and in the process I learned a valuable lesson about the ability of court pleadings and filings to bridge the gap between intention and realization—and even more about my own fascination with the law.

■ Because of my successes as an educator, the Peace Corps rewarded me with an optional third-year extension working in Zimbabwe's Division of Environment and Conservation office as a youth environmental officer. Seeing it as an excellent final step before law school, I jumped at the chance to work one more year in a capacity directly related to my career interests. I have spent the last year developing a national youth environmental program, serving as chairman of the Peace Corps Volunteer Advisory

Committee, and exploring the legal application of international environmental treaties, such as the Convention on Biodiversity, that Zimbabwe is party to. Zimbabwe's growing population and crippled economy have made clearing precious veldt forests for agriculture a matter of necessity. I have therefore tried to understand how culturally sensitive local legislation could be created that addresses both the economic and health interests of the country while fulfilling its obligation to international biodiversity convention mandates.

■ When I took my first private sector job at *Zone Digital*, I made the case to management that the magazine should boost its community and volunteer efforts. Good public relations, I reasoned, involved projecting a good public image, and so with my self-created charter in place, I set out to meet with various local nongovernment organizations (NGOs) to determine how we could work together in pro bono partnerships. I organized the first *Zone Digital* delegation to participate in the San Jose Cancer Walk, a fund-raising and awareness-generating walk through the city, and secured a major corporate donation to the charity. I also initiated a rewarding mentor relationship between *Zone Digital* and WirelessLearning, a nonprofit community education project in Mountain View. Working with WirelessLearning's director, we created a buddy system in which I arranged for the kids from WirelessLearning to meet the editors at *Zone Digital* to find out how they could best prepare for a career in multimedia. We also offered WirelessLearning a boost by profiling it in the magazine as an organization that was making a difference in the lives of urban youth.

- I'm particularly proud of the policy change I implemented last year in the Dover Free Clinic's treatment of strep throat. This disease can cause a sore throat in children, but more importantly it can also cause heart damage. Treating it effectively and quickly is critical. While the previous clinic policy, drug treatment, was effective, the drug's high cost meant that we could rarely get enough donations from pharmaceutical companies to serve our population. I researched the medical literature and consulted with infectious disease specialists and local epidemiologists as well as with the state public health department. Armed with my findings, I convinced the clinic to change the protocol from the expensive drug to a much cheaper but equally efficacious one that was available in a generic form and that pharmaceutical companies were much happier to donate in larger quantities.

Chapter 7 Perfect Phrases for Interests, Hobbies, and Passions

"In an essay of about 300 words, describe your passions and special interests."

(Illinois)

"The personal statements can be an opportunity to illuminate your intellectual background and interests."

(Harvard)

Another way to show schools who you are is to describe the activities that excite you the most. Passion and interest essay topics invite you to do just that. Whether your extracurricular interests center on rugby, haiku, or astrophysics, you want essays of this type to vividly communicate your love—and why you feel it. Some applicants' passion is no mere extracurricular hobby, but a larger calling, such as a social impact activity or even their profession. All these types of perfect phrases are illustrated in the following examples.

■ To satisfy my growing curiosity, later that year I served a paralegal internship on Dr. Ann Dravecky's Prison Law Project, sponsored by Brown's Legal Resources Consortium. For 13 weeks, I provided legal information to Rhode Island's growing and often ignored inmate population. Inmates who claimed they were wrongfully convicted would ask me about specific cases or to help them find relevant code, statutes, or cases. Managing about 25 cases at a time, I spent hours poring over penal codes and immersed in Internet research and used my weekends to hunt down case law in the library. I loved the hunt, but the emotional demands of corresponding with these prisoners over their often horrific cases sometimes gave me a queasy feeling. I did my best to assume they might in fact be wrongfully accused of the crimes they were convicted of, but that innocence often seemed quite unlikely. Was I working just as hard to help these almost certainly guilty prisoners as I was for those whose crimes were less serious or whose innocence seemed more plausible? The question seemed crucial.

■ The beauty and complexity of salsa was unlike anything I had ever experienced. After completing my Introduction to Dance class, I built on my rudimentary knowledge of salsa by taking lessons twice a week at a local dance school. The first three months of lessons were excruciatingly difficult, but I persevered until

I achieved a level of expertise that enabled me to dance with almost anyone. As soon as I was confident of my ability, I began taking my skills into the "real world" by going to Latin clubs such as the Copacabana, Latin Quarter, and El Flamingo. Naturally, I stand out at these clubs but regard comments such as, "Bailas bien para un Gringo"—"You dance well for a gringo"—as the highest of compliments.

- Latin is dauntingly complex. Compared to the 3 noun and 4 verb endings in English, Latin nouns have more than 30 endings indicating the word's function, and verbs claim approximately 100 endings. The language's flexible word structure, lengthy sentences, and intricate grammar combine to pose an intellectual challenge tailor-made for my memorization skills, mental dexterity, and analytical ability. The more I studied Latin, the more I enjoyed logically pulling apart even the most complex passages, extricating the individual pieces, and reordering them correctly to achieve a literal translation and a raw kind of sense. To truly understand Latin, however, I knew I had to look beyond the deciphered words at what the author really wanted to say. Only by analyzing the context and thrust of Catullus or Horace could I turn a literal translation into a fully human, fully nuanced act of expression.

- It was the Australian interior's very size and solitariness that pulled me in. So in 2005 I left the ocean behind and ventured into the outback to meet "real" Australians, encounter aboriginal culture, and discover the physical beauty of places like Uluru (the aboriginal name for Ayer's Rock) and King's Canyon. The sparseness of traffic on Australia's single-lane dirt roads occasionally left me stranded without food and forced me to spend the night in the desert under the southern stars. But I toughed it out, saw the beauty of the aborigines' decorative paintings, and watched as they performed their tribal dances to the accompaniment of their didgeridoos. Three weeks later I strolled exultantly into Perth.

- The patent approval process is my passion. During the 18-month process of back-and-forth negotiation with the patent attorney, we cite patent case law to each other to reshape the language of the patent application so it reflects the broadest interpretation of the technology's existing state of the art while remaining narrow enough to stay within the bounds of the inventive concept. I'm fascinated by the fact that the fate of an application can hinge on the appropriate or inappropriate placement of a single word in the would-be patent. Naturally, if a patent is issued with excessively broad language, it invites unnecessary litigation by other inventors who can claim that their ideas have been infringed upon. It's my job to see that this doesn't happen—and I love every minute of it.

- Carnatic music is one of the best known of the many ancient forms of Indian classical music. Consisting mainly of devotional songs composed centuries ago to praise the many Hindu gods or to pray for health, peace, and wealth, Carnatic music synchronizes my body and mind and helps me assimilate and enjoy the experiences of my life. Accompanying instruments such as the violin and miruthangam (a percussion instrument) add flavor to this vocal music, but it can be just as expressive and moving on its own. It encourages soul-searching and helps me find balance between temptations and the rational calm that should govern life. I've found that Carnatic music can even promote a feeling of family peace and warmth. When this other-worldly music is in the air, I can almost feel "goodness" entering our home and hearts.

- I had joined the Bureau of Land Management's Student Conservation Association summer volunteer program to get back to my first love, the environment, and reflect on the career focus that had so far eluded me. Although as a volunteer I performed a variety of tasks, surveying endangered tree frog populations fired my imagination like nothing else. These fascinating and fragile creatures were disappearing at an alarming rate because of the relentless destruction of their old-growth forest habitat. The Endangered Species Act mandated that government agencies (including BLM) do everything possible to save this animal and preserve its endangered home, but so far the logging companies were winning. Knowing that my field observations provided raw data that conservationists could use to save these majestic forests, I burned with frustration as I watched them get consigned to oblivion.

- In the language of an introductory psychology textbook, you could say I have a high need for cortical arousal. Though I have long been addicted to cycling, skiing, travel, rock climbing, photography, and flying, my recreational interests tend to morph and diversify. When I first started flying Cessnas, for example, airport-hopping the Southwest United States with my Canon SLR in tow met my definition of bliss. Two years later, however, I graduated to aerobatic flying and digital videography—which I combined to create adventure flying DVDs for friends.

- Outside of work I race cars—fast cars. Cars with 24-valve V–6 engines bored out of 3 liters to even 3.3 liters and force-fed with a Paxton supercharger dialed to produce 11 pounds of compressed-air—a boost so hot you need an intercooler mounted on the front to dissipate the heat. The cars I race have suspensions so stiff that my brain literally rattles inside my helmet if I hit so much as an occasional rock on the racetrack, and tires so sticky you'd swear they were made out of chewing gum.

Racing is a passion of mine not only for the adrenaline rush, but because of the way it heightens my senses, my mind, and my agility. In a sport where winners are decided by differences of less than 1/100 of a second and where you must react immediately to changing track conditions, racing has greatly sharpened my focus, reaction time, and ability to make split-second decisions.

Pashto became my passion. After earning a bachelor's in linguistics at Arizona State, I returned to Afghanistan after graduation to teach English in Kabul and pursue the holy grail of native fluency. Working freelance translating agricultural manuals from English into Pashto for a Kabul publisher and interpreting for U.S. soldiers stationed in Kandahar deepened my fascination for this poor, troubled, but culturally rich country divided by two tongues and multiple tribes. And gradually true fluency came. After three years of going native, my disclosure that I was actually a foreigner from the United States was increasingly met by protests that I must certainly have grown up in Afghanistan or had Pashtun parents. Eight years after entering Dr. Khattak's class, I had achieved my goal. When the Central Intelligence Agency hired me to translate intelligence feeds, I became the only American on a team of native Pashtun translators.

- Mary was scandalized. A senior teacher on our staff named Martha had just advised this young colleague of mine to abandon teaching, using exactly the same argument Martha had given me during a career counseling chat two years before: Mary was starting to enjoy herself too much! I sympathized with Mary's shock, but I understood Martha's wisdom with crystal clarity: the fulfillment of teaching is addictive, and like all addictions it can be very difficult to break. Whether I am teaching reading skills to my young students at Ferry Elementary or instructing school district administrators in the latest classroom technologies, teaching stimulates me intellectually and emotionally, gives me the special satisfaction of public "performance," deepens my capacity to build rapport with people from every background, and enables me to positively affect the lives of my students and the community as a whole. That is a powerful, even "addictive," mixture.

- I originally got involved in community service activities at Texas Tech to satisfy my parents' expectations. Cofounding Tech's Pet Fanciers Club, I recruited 78 members to sponsor dog and cat shows in the Lubbock area, and twice a month I tutored high school students in the inner city. Enjoying the way volunteer groups spawn friendships and a feeling of accomplishment, in my sophomore year I led six

➡

students in organizing events that raised $5,000 for The Safe Place, a nonprofit group that provides shelter and support for runaway teens. By my junior year, I was volunteering to be a dorm advisor, even over my parents' protests that it would take too much time away from my studies. Creating a "social impact" theme on my floor of 30 residents, I organized over six trips to food banks, elementary schools, and nursing homes. By my senior year the community life that had begun out of obedience to my parents had blossomed into an internship for U.S. Congressman Randy Neugebauer, for whom I handle social-work cases involving worker's comp, food stamps, and unemployment training.

■ It was during the second month of my Peace Corps stint in Sironko, Uganda, that Fabayo, our office's maid and cook, mentioned that she was sending her eight-year-old son, Adofo, to work for a blacksmith. I tried to picture little Adofo engulfed in the heat and hazard of a blacksmith's shop and was appalled. Always struggling on their $400 annual income, Fabayo and her husband, a carpenter, had already pulled four of their children out of school so they could learn trades to support themselves. Now Adofo was to be the fifth. Since Fabayo and her husband's parents had done the same to them, they simply had no idea that staying in school might earn their children even better livelihoods as adults. Because the schools in Sironko could not teach the community's children for free and most poor families could not afford the tuition, I decided to organize free elementary education classes for kids like Adofo. First, I created an infrastructure—classrooms, teachers, books—by making strategic donations to locals in exchange for use of a makeshift classroom and the part-time teaching assistance of a nearby missionary organization. Three weeks after conceiving my plan, the Sironko school started class with seven children.

- When I was 18, two friends and I jumped on a Greyhound bus and spent eight weeks traveling through California, Nevada, Utah, and Wyoming. My love for Native American art is the result. I immediately identified with the emphasis Hopi, Navaho, and Zuni Indians place on worshipping nature and community. The beautiful artwork, ceramics, and statuary that reflect that sacred vision charmed and fascinated me like nothing I'd seen before. Today, my apartment is chock full of Native American blankets, pottery, and figures, and last fall I proudly launched NativeArtWays.org, a blog and trading platform for native art connoisseurs.

- I may be the only art history major who can say he really loves math. With its proofs and rigorous logic, math is a system of simple rules—like the law—that are developed and combined to create a more complex system. In mathematics you must prove theorems assumed to be true by applying definitions and other theorems in such a way that you conclusively show that your theorem is correct and, given the specific circumstances of your "case," will always produce the same conclusion. This parallels the application of case law, and if I had to identify what it is that draws me to the law as magnetically as to math, it's the intellectual rigor.

Chapter 8 Perfect Phrases for Diversity Essays

"The statement should describe any unusual aspects of your background that might provide an element of diversity at Emory Law."

(Emory)

"While admission to Stanford Law School is based primarily upon superior academic achievement and potential to contribute to the legal profession, the Admissions Committee also regards the diversity of an entering class as important to the school's educational mission. If you would like the committee to consider how factors such as your background, life and work experiences, advanced studies, extracurricular or community activities, culture, socio-economic status, sex, race, ethnicity, religion, or sexual orientation would contribute to the diversity of the entering class and hence to your classmates' law school experience, please describe these factors and their relevance."

(Stanford)

Law schools want diverse classes—period. Fortunately, they define "diversity" quite loosely. Aside from race and gender, your personal or family history, your religion and cultural background, your international and travel experiences, your hobbies and passions, even your sexuality (if handled properly) are all fair game as diversity essay topics. Indeed, diversity is such a critical topic that many schools invite applicants to submit an essay exclusively on that topic in addition to their personal statement. Let's look at some perfect phrases for diversity. Because previous chapters have provided perfect phrases for diversity-as-broadly-defined, in this chapter we emphasize perfect phrases for cross-cultural and ethnic diversity.

- Sometimes the best way to understand the society you belong to is to leave it. Moving with my parents to Warsaw when I was seven gave me an early and intense curiosity about cultural dissimilarities that I still possess after living in five cities on four continents. Why do Norwegians toast so formally? Why do Turks waste so much water? Why are chopsticks plastic in Chinese restaurants, metal in Korea, and wood everywhere else? The 16 years I've spent living, traveling, and working outside the United States have helped me answer some of these questions, and in doing so understand myself and America better. Because I finally define myself as American, I am returning to the United States to earn my ⮕

law degree. But I'll never forget that it's the perspective I've gained living in Brazil, Sudan, Korea, and Germany that gives me the confidence to make that decision.

- During the day I may look the part of a successful corporate "suit," but I doubt my P&G officemates would recognize me in my off-hours identity: busker and troubadour. Last week, I played my second gig at Coffee Stages, a coffeehouse-cum-music club on Chicago's north side. I've performed at open mikes like this one, on and off, for roughly eight years, and in fact have just recorded my first MP3, for release on my Web site, www.MattBrendMusic.com. Still, the highlight of my musical career came while backpacking through Europe in 2005. At dusk one night on the steps of Madrid's eighteenth-century Monasterio de la Encarnación, I connected with two buskers I heard playing Coldplay tunes on their guitars. Though we couldn't speak each others' languages, we shared musical tastes and a common repertoire. After jamming for hours, they invited me to follow them south to the historic city of Toledo to play in a street musician's festival. For four days, the four of us bounced Radiohead, Coldplay, and Björk tunes off the cobbled walkways and alcoves of this ancient and beautiful town, at times before crowds of 20 to 30 townspeople.

- I never expected to "come out" to my coworkers at Home Depot. But when volunteering to conduct an AIDS awareness training program for our regional field offices, my manager casually asked me the reason for my interest, and I decided to tell him. For the next eight weeks as I conducted corporate training programs across the organization, I was greeted everywhere I went with gestures of interest, support, and tolerance. But the real gratification came in the months that followed, when the corporate newsletter ran a sensitivity-building article about same-sex relationships, and I began seeing notices for gay/lesbian affinity group meetings on the corporate intranet. My decision to get involved in a way that aligns with my sexuality had indirectly helped to open dialogue about gay and lesbian issues among Home Depot employees. That knowledge has emboldened me to take my advocacy to a new level.

■ The Farmers Credit Bank (FCB) branch where I interned at the University of Oklahoma had 100 employees, and every single one was white and born in Oklahoma. Diversity did not exist. In my opinion it is no coincidence that this same bank had so flagrantly ignored northeast Oklahoma's rapidly growing Hispanic population that its regional market share fell from second to fifth in only five years. In a corporate culture still ruled by a parochial, small-town mindset, pushing for innovation seemed pointless. Shortly after my graduation I left Broken Arrow and my comfortable, low-risk job at FCB for a position in the commercial retail division of Citibank

Miami. Twice a week I found myself seated around a large conference table with bank employees from 12 nations discussing how to market the bank's new personal finance products to the Florida, Caribbean, and South American markets. Because I had arrived fluent in Spanish, by my second month I had the authority to make personal marketing calls to individual South American bankers. Unlike FCB, Citibank sought out reasons to change in order to meet the market rather than reasons to avoid it. As my diverse colleagues discussed our excellent sales results in Puerto Rico, Costa Rica, and Colombia, for the first time in my life I was an enthused, complete person. I believe the proactive innovation and cultural openness I have experienced (and demonstrated) at Citibank prove the power of diversity as a leadership tool. But to begin to wield that tool, I needed to move to Citibank's diversity-embracing culture. I choose to earn my law degree at Columbia for precisely the same reason.

- Greenpeace is a truly multinational organization: my boss is Dutch, his boss is Irish, and the executive director is German. Every day I work with individuals from Hong Kong, Argentina, Holland, Great Britain, Germany, Nigeria, and Switzerland. Because of my effectiveness in working with such diverse teams and my track record for getting results, in 2007 Greenpeace invited me to participate in its worldwide IMPACT initiative to build leadership and change-management skills among Greenpeace's regional directors. I was assigned to work with Greenpeace Malaysia's director and six country managers to develop a new system for building membership and media visibility through Internet and wireless technologies. As part of this change process, I had to build and work continuously with a functionally diverse team of people from such areas as law, marketing, technology, and planning. Diversity was not a "value-add" in this project—it was its heart.

- The cultural open-mindedness that informed my decision to spend a year with the Karanga-Rozvi tribe is the direct result of my international upbringing and my parents' unrelenting efforts to expose my brother, Nir, and me to the cuisine, customs, and lifestyles of other cultures. Growing up as part of the U.S. Navy's extended overseas family at Yokosuka, Japan, and Naples, Italy, I had limitless opportunities to immerse myself in two of the world's richest cultures. While many military-base residents tended to turn inward, succumbing early to "island fever," my parents busily interacted with the local gentry, exploring local groceries and merchants, learning the language with the gusto of immigrants with no home to return to, and inviting locals into our living room for weekly English lessons. In Yokosuka, this meant Nir and I gained extensive face time with

➡

Japanese children, which eventually triggered our rabid efforts to build the largest collections of Manga, Anime, and Tamiya auto and robot model kits outside of Greater Nippon.

- For Dr. Shelby it was an article of faith that one-dimensional teams produce ordinary results. Valuation, litigation, and forensic (VLF) consultancies usually employ MBAs and CFAs, but Gunnardson Jones employs J.D.s, Ph.D.s, and others—anything to enrich the perspectives we can bring to clients. For example, our former manager, Martha, was raised in South Africa, graduated from NYU Law School, and practiced bankruptcy law for 10 years. Paul, our part-time senior analyst, was born in São Paulo, is fluent in Portuguese and Farsi, graduated from University of Michigan Law School, and is currently a Ph.D. student at Columbia. And I, former analyst and now a manager, was raised in Honolulu, educated in Texas in the methods of scientific analysis, and trained in the trenches of valuation, finance, and economics. Believe me, for a VLS firm that is serious diversity.

- After the 9/11 attack in New York, Anaheim's Muslim community gained attention it did not want or deserve. Overnight, my non-Muslim neighbors became suspicious of the entire Muslim community, though until then we had lived peacefully with each other on the same streets for years. The 9/11 backlash was severe. I can still remember hearing my non-Muslim next-door neighbor tell me that his mother had proclaimed that henceforth no more Muslims would enter her house, though her own daughter had married one! Even in my own workplace, I noticed a new wariness and self-segregation divide our Muslim and non-Muslim workforce. Eager to prevent this poisoning of a once-collegial workplace, I decided to invite our six Muslim employees to my house for a weekend World Series party. Though some were initially reluctant, all six came, and over the course of four hours' food and conversation we grew closer. When MediTherapeutics suffered its first war casualty—our sales manager's enlisted son lost his life in Fallujah—our Muslim colleagues were the first to offer Rick their condolences and support.

- As a Mexico-trained criminal investigator, I can bring a singular perspective to my George Washington University classes. After learning the principles and methods of criminal investigation at Universidad Panamericana in Mexico City, I began my career investigating violent murders for Puebla State's detective squad. I still remember the day my team and I learned that a murderer responsible for the rape and murder of three prostitutes was hiding at a local school. We were all horrified at the thought of the danger the children might be in, but, putting our emotions aside, we applied our analytical and team skills and captured the murderer at the time and location our deductive training had told us to expect. In those 18 months I gained insights into criminal behavior and investigation, Mexico's justice system, and the power of teamwork that will enrich my international law classes at GWU.

- The diversity I offer Cornell Law is based on four unique elements of my life: my professional experiences in corporate finance and the hospitality industry; my appreciation of the Persian, Kurd, and American cultures that define me; my quantitatively rigorous education and graduate research work at MIT; and my efforts to fight discrimination based on sexual orientation. For me, culture shock—experiencing the foreign in sometimes jarring ways—has been a natural part of doing business internationally. Such "shock" does not need to be traumatic or unpleasant. Quite the contrary.

- The Israeli army is a melting pot of people from virtually every imaginable background and race. As an officer, the division I led consisted of two Poles, four Moroccans, one Hungarian, two Russians, two Germans, two Iraqis, one Yemeni, and one Egyptian. Such diversity is not unusual. To foster a sense of teamwork in this heterogeneous society, I learned to create opportunities for communication and to nurture each individual's sense of uniqueness. After I had finished my training as a rookie officer, I joined a department where two Russian-born soldiers had fallen behind the others professionally and socially because of their poor Hebrew skills. I convinced two other soldiers to join me in teaching the language to them, and they quickly got the hang of it and began to integrate into the group. Soon other soldiers were volunteering to take a part in our educational operation. Five months later, the two Russian soldiers were promoted to managerial positions. I'll bring this same instinct to reach across cultural barriers to my Stanford Law classmates.

- As a son of a French-trained World Bank expert in animal genetics, I had an international life virtually from birth. I spent my first five years in a diverse, multilingual research community in Azerbaijan where my friends and neighbors ranged from Azerbaijanis and Russians to Brits and Indians. When I was 6 we moved back to Kuala Lumpur, but I continued to seek out international experiences. At 14, I served as a cultural guide for the Burmese team in the All-South Asian Games, meeting people from all over the continent. When I was 16 I spent a summer in London working for McDonald's, where I gained my first lesson in business and interacted with people from the United States, France, Brazil, and Holland. When I moved to New York City for college, I immediately felt at home in Manhattan's world-embracing diaspora. I want to learn and practice the law of the United States because its "melting pot" culture matches the substance and spirit of my "melting pot" life.

- While touring a production line on a business trip to Quebec in 2007, I noticed that my colleagues became much more willing to share information the moment I began conversing with them in French. People are simply more receptive to everything, from a compliment to a suggestion, when it is given in their mother tongue. Today, I'm excited to be adding proficiency in Mandarin to my fluency in French, Greek, and English so I can build on the rapport I've developed with my new Chinese colleagues. The power one gains by understanding a foreign language cannot be understated.

- Growing up in four different regions of the vast Russian subcontinent, working with Scandinavians and South Americans in London, forming a soccer team in the American Deep South—wherever I have been, I have promoted exploration, open-mindedness, and personal challenge as my guiding principles. I will make a real contribution to UCLA because my spirit of discovery is infectious, and my experiences have taught me a great deal about working effectively with others.

- The world is shrinking; economies and markets inexorably converge. Every individual and every society must discover its own way to celebrate this convergence while preserving—and celebrating—its own identity and uniqueness. At Vanderbilt University Law School I will seek this perfect middle ground between unity and diversity in everything I do. I look forward to sharing with my classmates my belief in the kind of integrity that remains true to traditional values and cultural heritage.

Chapter 9 Perfect Phrases for Goals and Why Law School

"We encourage you to discuss personal and professional goals that are important to you."

(Northwestern)

"Please discuss why you wish to study law. Please note that the Admissions Committee is interested in your answer to this specific question and a general personal statement will not suffice."

(University of Connecticut)

L aw schools do not expect the majority of applicants, especially those applying directly out of college, to use their personal statements to provide a full-fledged post-J.D. career plan. They understand that even applicants with some law-related coursework and work experience are not likely to have fully formed career plans. (Even if they did, they are not likely to write about them in insightful or engaging ways.) It's because law schools see so many uninformative "I've always wanted to be a lawyer" essays that your best strategy is to focus your personal statement on something other than the law, bringing it in, if at all, only at the end.

Still, you may be one of the applicants who actually does know why he wants a J.D., has "due-diligenced" his legal career, and can speak about the law in substantive ways. Or you may have devoted your personal statement to stories unrelated to the law but want to focus your optional or secondary essay on your post-J.D. goals. If so, the perfect phrases in this chapter are for you. We've divided them into three categories—perfect phrases describing the journey that brought applicants to the decision to go to law school, those describing specific post-J.D. goals, and those about the applicants' specific reasons for choosing a particular law school.

Journey to the Law

- "Hey, keep it down!" The school kids giggled as the smiling old man with the funny hat—some librarian or crazy person no doubt—called to them from the Supreme Court's marble hallway. Though teachers always recognized him, the students rarely realized that the cranky denizen hailing them was the late Chief Justice Rehnquist on his morning walk around the building. As a summer intern at the U.S. Supreme Court, every day I earned extraordinary insights into the people behind the law. Like a chief justice masquerading as a crotchety custodian, "The Law," I learned, is not always what it seems. It encompasses much more than marble halls, judicial robes, and grave decorum. For example, when the Clerk of the Court, Major General William Suter, encouraged me to apply, I learned that one of my highest duties as an intern was to uphold the image of the court. I would never have guessed that the highest court's august image needed protecting! Yet I soon discovered that the office was regularly besieged by slightly unstable petitioners upset that a justice could not intervene to resolve their child custody battle or reverse their auto repossession. It was because of this sometimes amusing reality behind the hall of justice's polished brass and marble that the stern environment I had imagined quickly metamorphosed into a warm family: four fellow interns and the friendly permanent staff. Though there was certainly some "glamour"—fielding research requests from *New York Times* reporters, for example, or watching Justice Thomas drive up in his car—much of my internship was spent in a cramped, sterilely lit paper factory known as the Records and Archives Area—an environment immediately recognizable to anyone who's ever worked in a corporate office. In short, my time at the Supreme Court differed from my expectations—including in its impact on my career choices.

- When I began my nine-week internship at the Democratic National Committee, the only person I knew in Washington was my former dorm mate, who now worked at a semiadult video store on U Street. Yet walking around Capitol Hill with a research pass to the Library of Congress I felt like the future of The Republic somehow depended on my menial research assignments. When some material on Republican tax breaks for the rich made it onto a CNN report, my self-pride became insufferable. Meeting Dawn Machado, a legislative aide for Representative Sanchez of South Florida, changed everything. As we debated the hot issues—Iraq, the Obama-McCain race, the economy— over lattes, I realized how little I really knew about the way Washington worked. As she introduced me to lobbyists, journalists, academics, and politicians, my naïveté and self-regard fell away, leaving only fascination and a desire to learn and do more. Dawn became my mentor, confidante, and confessor, and when she one day told me I had the intellectual "chops" to build a career in government, I began to seriously consider law school.

- The education I get every day at the Patent and Trademark Office is not limited to researching technology's bleeding edge. I also get to learn from the styles, tactics, and strategies of some of the world's brightest attorneys. Interacting with legal counsel for

➡

the PTO and intellectual property law firms around the nation has helped me understand the intricacies of Title 35 of the U.S Code (federal patent law). Today, I move comfortably between procedural and substantive law, statutory and case law. As an associate member of the Government Patent Lawyers Association, I have been fortunate to become acquainted with such outstanding patent lawyers as Alfred Beersman, a PTO administrative patent judge, and J. Michael Schulz, a patent attorney at the Department of Energy. They have encouraged me to earn the law degree that will enable me to optimize my skills and impact and ultimately, I hope, rise to a patent judgeship on the PTO's Patent Board of Appeals.

■ Umpiring was my first hard lesson in conflict resolution and my first inkling that I enjoyed working with kids. The kids were fine—it was the parents who made me earn my pay. They yelled and screamed constantly at me, sure that they knew all the rules, though I was the only one who read the 80-page rule book before every game. I quickly learned that the only way I would be able to control the parents was to know the rule book well enough to cite every rule from memory. In a way, umpiring was the same kind of work I enjoy today at Atlanta's Office of Juvenile Defenders—helping kids in a challenging environment where a passion for the laws of that "environment" is crucial.

- When the law school of Luiss University, one of Italy's two best private institutions, offered me a position teaching advanced-level English to law students, I realized that I needed to be prepared to discuss legal issues. I began reading books on law; the more I read, the more interesting I found it, and the more I wanted to learn. The elegant clarity of legal thinking and the ordered reasoning of its argumentation fascinated me. As I read lawyers and judges making analogies and using language so eloquently and gracefully I also began to see how creative law can be. I wanted to learn as much as possible and eagerly read books about any legal subject. While doing so, I began to research gender-related legal issues and began to see the direct links between the law and the inequalities faced by women in Italy and other parts of the world. A career in law began to crystallize as the best way for me to use my talents, do something that fascinated me, and work for a larger cause—women's rights—at the same time.

- Tim Weisberg, an attorney and family friend, is the reason I want to pursue a law career. Five years ago my mother put up a tortilla stall in front of her Mexican restaurant in Taos to serve the torrent of visitors she expected for the city's annual Art Days parade. Although she owns a year-round business, the city tried to subject her to a municipal ordinance that applies to traveling, temporary vendors whose stalls typically line

Civic Plaza Drive for the parade. The situation came to a head when three uniformed police officers attempted to arrest my mother in her restaurant's kitchen as she frantically prepared her menu for the first day of the festival. Buying herself time by convincing the constabulary that she would "turn herself in" when the parade was over, my mother did just that the next morning, bringing Tim and me along for support. That's when it happened. Tim, a Las Vegas corporate attorney who doesn't even practice in New Mexico, patiently negotiated with the city officials, brilliantly diffusing the tense situation. Gently but firmly, without provocation or threat, he suggested they had used "SWAT team" tactics in arresting my mother and had, in any case, misinterpreted Taos's city vending code. The police apologized and set us free. My mother's tortilla stand has been an Art Days parade fixture ever since, and, after clerking for Tim's firm last summer, I have decided to do my best to emulate him in using reason and interpersonal skills to defend my clients' rights as a practicing attorney.

- Maryland's Environmental Services Agency had hired me initially for a summer project to investigate suspected pollution sources in Chesapeake Bay. Because I was able to identify two of the three contamination sources, that fall they asked me to continue on a contract basis as a technical consultant.

As much as I enjoyed the purely field-based environmental work, I was surprised to find I particularly enjoyed writing the plans, applications, and grants that enabled ESA to obtain more state and federal funding. When my first plan, for the application of biosolids to agricultural land remediation, was accepted without amendment, it felt as good as my first pinch-hit home run for the Towson University Tigers. My plan development work required me to research and understand the regulations of the Environmental Protection Agency and utilize a broad array of disciplines, from chemistry and geology to agriculture and regulatory law. By helping me see the vital role the law plays in managing our natural resources, my ESA position also helped me see that my future is the law.

■ The attorney told me that she had never heard of this "battery by gassing" charge before and wanted to know what legal history had earned it the status of a "wobbler" offense—one that could be charged as either a felony or a misdemeanor. I located the original wording of the proposed bill that sought to make "battery by gassing" a straight felony. Since it is currently a wobbler, it stood to reason that some legislative history had since changed "battery by gassing" into a misdemeanor. We were unable to find that case, so we argued that of all the bodily fluids that could be expunged, spit was one of the less offensive

➡

and thus Van Nguyen should be charged with a misdemeanor. It was a novel and fascinating case, and I loved every minute of it.

- It was during my internship at one of Germany's leading intellectual property (IP) law firms—Doehring, Apfel, Burnitz, & Dietz—in 2004 that I discovered the excitement and complexity of IP and media law. Working on copyright infringement cases, applications to transfer IP-related rights, and entertainment and media contracts, I saw that IP law would enable me to combine my knowledge of technology with my international experiences in an area of the law that is changing faster than virtually any other specialization. The more I learned about IP law, the more I became fascinated with the way the changing nature of intellectual property is forcing the world's legal systems to reinvent themselves. I began to envision a career in this critical new field.

- The more I thought about the hard work my campus security team had invested in finding and shutting down the campus meth lab, the more empty and uncertain that accomplishment began to seem. Wasn't Chief Dyson's, "We did *our* jobs" just a cop-out, a washing of hands of moral responsibility? After all, weeks later, 12 jurors would scrutinize our actions in court to decide whether we had made the correct choices. How would they judge us, I wondered? Would they decide we had acted competently? Would the perpetrators even be convicted? As gratified as I was to be part of law enforcement, these questions bothered me, precisely because I had learned how much is truly beyond police officers' control. For me, enforcing laws was no longer enough.

- Intent on making our computer system installation a success, I conducted an extensive search and selection process, informed the winning vendor, and awaited his contract in the mail. When I received it, I was shocked by its brevity, given the magnitude of our purchase. When I forwarded it to our attorney, Steve Martucci, he explained that the contract was short because it lacked provisions protecting our company if problems or delays arose. Steve involved me deeply in the process of drawing up addenda for the document, asking me for my input on the issues that would affect us most if the computer system disappointed. I was fascinated by the complexity of the drafting process as well as by the way Steve's exacting language covered us precisely as much as we needed to be covered. Though the president of the computer company was less than thrilled at the significantly more detailed contract we returned to him, he signed it, and in the weeks that followed I began to work more closely with Steve on all the legal issues that involved my company. That initial exposure to the law has bloomed into a new career direction.

- After graduation, I came to Washington to put my political science degree to work as Congressman Ned Forbes's legislative aide and, ultimately, as chief of staff for Congressman Blake Sturtevant. As a legislative assistant to two Ohio congressmen, I had to be ready to leap from issue to issue depending on the committees they were assigned to. But Social Security remained the issue closest to my heart. Under Congressman Sturtevant, I drafted Social Security Administration–related amendments, prepared questions for witnesses before his Labor, Health, and Human Services Subcommittee, and established legislative priorities for him on Social Security and retirement issues in liaison with the Office of the Deputy Commissioner for Legislation and Congressional Affairs. My role in achieving passage of H.R. 3963, Children's Health Insurance Program Reauthorization Act of 2007 (also known as "SCHIP"), on October 25, 2007, was the deciding factor in my decision to pursue a career in politics, which I believe must begin with a law degree.

- As a patent technology scientist in Aztec Lab's patent department, I found a unique way to begin building a bridge between my love for biotechnology and my growing fascination with intellectual property issues. Over the past 12 months, I have performed prior art and freedom-to-operate searches in collaboration with

Aztec's staff patent attorneys and scientists and used intellectual property and scientific databases to analyze infringement and validity issues for three medical and molecular devices. My patent intelligence and analysis work has supported four key Aztec licensing, acquisitions, and business development initiatives that represent millions of dollars in potential biotechnology revenues. The capstone event for me was leading the three-person patent intelligence support team for Aztec's new potential blockbuster cancer drug, Ocravitin.

■ My broad responsibilities as Google's business development manager exposed me to new business functions, including the law. Almost daily I was negotiating some sort of agreement, which I would codify into contracts together with our staff attorneys. As I developed new products and found new partners, I often consulted with our lawyers about copyright issues pertaining to localization and the syndication of translated text images and video. Moreover, my interaction with foreign lawyers gave me a glimpse into comparative law. I enjoyed the rigor and precision of the law, the elegance of its terms of art, and its awe-inspiring internal logic. Above all, I enjoyed the raw intelligence and intellectual agility of its practitioners. I felt that they thought like I did, could see the patterns and ramifications that others missed, brought to their

➡

craft some of the "pleasure of the mind" that I had not felt since graduate school.

■ Professor Nord's agricultural law class reopened my mind to the world of torts, contracts, and real estate that I had first encountered during my father's front-porch conversations with the ranch attorney, Bob McCarthy. With Dr. Nord's nuanced guidance, legal issues I once had thought cut and dried—rights to deeded water sources or contract "violations" by feed suppliers—now contained vast gray areas open to interpretation and discrimination. Where I had once considered the law an arcane nuisance, I now saw that it was the underpinning of literally every issue of importance to the ranch, from labor contracts with our ranch hands and property issues involving cattle and equipment to the complicated legal problems posed by our need to expand our range land eastward. To my surprise I found researching Wyoming's ranch case law almost as much fun as roping a steer at the 2004 Wrangler National Finals. For good or bad, the days when a handshake sealed the deal are long gone in Wyoming. More and more, the future of the Bucking T Ranch will depend on a sound and proactive understanding of the law.

■ In my final semester at Alabama State I decided to try an elective on dispute resolution. Alice Knightman, the attorney who taught the class, was well regarded by Jefferson County judges for her successes in handling complex contract and family law issues, and in class she was inspiringly passionate about both the art and the utility of dispute resolution as a substitute for lengthy proceedings. Working on mock arbitration projects in her class, I began to see the almost uncanny connections between the work mediators perform and my interests, skills, and professional experiences as a family counselor. Just like a mediator, I have to make counteroffers and suggestions to push parties closer to resolution, and just as with dispute resolution, finding and pushing my clients toward Solomonic compromises is a key skill.

■ The law I glimpsed as a Congressional page—as an imposing public edifice, as the ceremonial application of formal procedures—does not attract me. In accompanying my uncle on a business trip for his corporate law firm in Asia last year, I discovered a different side of the law, one of human give and take and subtle behind-the-scenes preparations, negotiations, counterresponses. This law excites me and speaks to who I am. I watched my uncle draw out negotiations with a Korean shipbuilding firm for six months just so he could gauge and "position" it well as an opponent. I listened as he explained how a rather impressive (to me) presentation by a Hong Kong business partner was really just smoke and mirrors masking a hidden agenda. Through him, I saw the law

➡

as skillfully playing roles, assessing people, uncovering motivations, and negotiating from one's knowledge and instincts. It is this psychological, direct, and most human aspect of the law that appeals to me. I have been privileged to see many examples of it in my life—the powerful, charismatic tycoon Howard Drew listening intently and respectfully as my uncle explained the legal ramifications of a transaction; Werner Erdmann, former German economics minister and partner of my uncle, advising me to be like him and "get out dere und make dings happen"; or Chuck Wilde, a Los Angeles entertainment attorney, illustrating for me the dramatic differences between the East Coast and West Coast styles of law. I want to practice the people-focused law these role models know—not the governmental, public side of the law, but the law of the free market as it meets gritty reality and messy change. I want to experience the power of law as it moves, not in the stately, historically freighted way of the District Court of Appeals, but swiftly, personally, and tangibly in response to the very human people it serves.

Specific Goals

- It's no longer enough to be a "friend" of the environment, to volunteer regularly for the World Wildlife Fund, or even to use my natural resources

115

management degree in a public-sector administrative role. I need to contribute to the formation of natural resources policy, to enter the black box where all my environmental impact reports for the National Park Service have disappeared and escort them through the thickets of bureaucratic indifference and lobbyist self-interest to the resolution they deserve. I want to supplement and leverage my lifelong love of the environment and the scientific training I gained at the University of New Mexico by gaining a foundation in environmental law. As an attorney trained in environmental litigation techniques and case law as well as land and resource use issues, I can do more than sympathize and support environmental organizations working to protect endangered habitats and species. I can proactively advocate for them as a lawyer and policy maker.

- In 2004, I cofounded the U.S.-Vietnam Intellectual Property Consortium (USVIPC), a U.S.-based nonprofit organization whose mission is to work with the U.S. and Vietnamese governments to create the legal, political, and policy climate in Vietnam to create the intellectual property rights regime that will accelerate Vietnam's growth as an economic powerhouse in Southeast Asia. A J.D. in patent law and intellectual property will enable me to apply my technological expertise to practical IP work that will support my long-term efforts on behalf of USVIPC. Ultimately, I hope to join a global NGO such as the United Nations, ASEAN, or the World Bank in a special advisory role working to implement intellectual property principles in developing economies.

- My goal is to continue working for shareholders' rights but on a larger, national scale, drawing on my training as a financial analyst to identify situations where minority shareholders have been abused and need a proactive advocate. Although my initial efforts with small and middle-tier corporations in the Des Moines area have been successful, if I intend to challenge more sophisticated corporations, I know I will require a thorough immersion in the law, including the principles of fiduciary duty, securities regulation, negotiation, and of course litigation. After earning my J.D., I'll begin expanding my shareholder advocacy skills by working through an activist investment fund or by joining a conventional law firm. Whichever specific path my career takes, I'll continue to fight for good corporate governance, the sine qua non behind American capitalism's role as the greatest force for ethical prosperity in the world.

- In the short term, I want to gain practical experience in tax law by working for a private entity, such as a law firm, that represents Russian companies doing business in the United States. When I have established myself as an experienced tax specialist, I will return to Russia and provide legal counsel in tax law to Russian companies seeking cross-border trade opportunities in the United States. My larger goal is to help promote international trade law by working to ensure that goods, services, and capital flow freely, fairly, and reciprocally between nations based on open-market principles.

- My vivid confrontations with the dislocations caused by globalization in places like Gambier, Ohio, have motivated me to bring together the two "personalities" of my career—business savvy and social justice, the world of corporations and of human beings. A J.D./MBA will give me the critical tools of law, policy making, and management to help mitigate the negative and promote the positive social impacts of the global economy. In the short term, I will use the broad skills I gain from a J.D./MBA to create new jobs and social wealth through private equity, specifically, by turning around failing firms through mergers and acquisitions. The J.D. in particular will give me the skills I will need to construct the complicated contracts required for successful transactions. In the long term, I will use the J.D. to focus increasingly on social issues, such as leading public-private partnerships like those I developed for the city of Toledo at Boston Consulting Group. Finally, because I hope to run for office one day, a J.D. will be an essential tool for crafting policies that improve government's interactions with business from a social and regulatory standpoint.

- My objective is to become a trial attorney who is capable of leveraging a sophisticated understanding of every facet of courtroom interaction. As an attorney with both psychological and legal training, I will be better able to systematically evaluate each element of a pending case and to know what interests, confuses, or persuades a jury before I go to trial. Eventually, I hope to know how a jury evaluates the judge's nonverbal communication and what affects a defendant's demeanor has on a juror's perceptions of credibility or guilt. When I frame an argument as an attorney, I want to have a comprehensive knowledge of the varied processes of jury decision making. Ultimately I aspire to be a respected trial lawyer in criminal law and to perhaps eventually take that experience into academia as a professor. I am also looking at possible careers in jury selection, image management, or trial strategy. Toward these ends, I intend to continue my education with the eventual objective of receiving both a J.D. and a Ph.D.

- After earning my master's I began my career as a tax accountant preparing taxes for individuals, corporations, and partnerships in the Rochester area. The complexity of the work I performed steadily increased, and in a matter of months, I was completing research and consulting work for partnerships and large, closely held corporations like Kodak and Birds Eye. Today, I analyze the tax implications of corporate transactions for United Technologies and perform tax consulting work for a local CPA firm. However, without a law degree the services in tax consulting and compliance I can provide my clients will remain limited. As an attorney I will be able to represent clients starting at the planning stages of an engagement (information gathering), then in the implementation stages (drafting legal documents), and finally, if needed, as a representative before government agencies and courts.

- Technology start-ups needing help with management, and financial and technology issues can choose from a welter of venture capitalists, strategic consulting companies, and technology consultants like myself. Yet too many of these companies will fail because they lack the legal expertise to protect their intellectual property, can't afford protracted litigation with a competitor, or can't find attorneys willing to receive equity stakes. For many technology start-ups legal expertise that is highly specialized to their needs is hard to find. There remains a market need for entrepreneur-friendly attorneys who have the technology industry experience and risk tolerance to provide sound legal counsel and representation to new technology ventures. Of course, many law firms have already targeted entrepreneurial ventures as a specialty or "boutique" market, but few of these focus specifically and exclusively on start-ups, and even fewer focus on start-ups that are not based in highly visible, saturated new-venture markets like Silicon Valley. Above all, fewer still have the hard entrepreneurial experience to truly understand the risks their clients are undertaking. Because I have that technology expertise and that entrepreneurial experience, I can begin filling this great market need— as soon as I earn my J.D.

- As gratifying as my volunteer work at Bethel Psychological Services has been, it pales in comparison to the impact I can have as an attorney protecting patients' rights. Working initially for a personal injury law firm, I will learn how to defend the interests of underrepresented mentally ill patients by ensuring that psychological or psychiatric treatment receives the same insurance coverage as purely physical conditions. Ten to fifteen years after my J.D., I intend to take my campaign to the policy-making side, as a state representative, a government agency director, or a lobbyist, to fight for parity between mental and physical ailments before the law.

- My dream remains a career in entertainment law or contract law. I want to use my unique knowledge of the recording industry from the performer's side to enlist and represent entertainment/media industry clients like my friends DJ Kid Noyze and Mos Thugg. As their agent, I will prepare and negotiate performance contracts and royalty, merchandising, licensing, distribution, and endorsement agreements, but I also look forward to proactively seeking out and structuring financing and marketing deals for them. To give myself the solid foundation to navigate the rapid changes taking place in media technologies, marketing, and finance, I will work for five years after my J.D. in a corporate finance law environment in order to give myself a firm understanding of corporate law basics and the Uniform Commercial Code. Eventually, I hope to start a Miami-based boutique entertainment law firm specializing in Hispanic hip-hop artists.

■ This traumatic experience confirmed my decision to pursue a career as a personal injury lawyer with a specialization in maritime law for a Southern California law firm serving cruise ship passenger and sea industry employee clients. Onboard accidents, infections, and rape are growing issues for the vacation cruise industry, and few cruise customers realize that admiralty or maritime law may govern their case depending on whether the incident occurs in international, U.S. coastal, or California territorial waters. Likewise, few seamen or longshoremen injured on the high seas, in inland waterways, or on harborside docks know the specialized law that governs their work environments. After 10 to 15 years gaining experience in maritime-related tort cases for law firms like Mossley, Flint & Schurz or Marriott Greenberg, I'll be ready to take over my father's practice in San Pedro when he retires.

- Capitalizing on my exposure to tax-related issues at Bryn Mawr and Deery Tax Partners, after I have earned my J.D. degree and passed the Massachusetts bar, I want to begin practicing estate planning as an attorney at a midsize Boston firm like Garrison Portnoy or Boylston Associates. Helping clients prepare and review wills, trusts, and other related documents will enable me to ensure that estate holders' wishes are honored by legally structured schemes. Through my expertise, clients will know that the beneficiaries they designate will truly benefit from their estate plans and that their estates will be distributed speedily, cost-effectively, and professionally.

- I want to combine my technical and legislative experience with a joint J.D./MBA degree so I can build a Web-based service that provides low-cost but reliable legal advice to the general consumer public. I envision a user-friendly, one-stop shop for basic legal services, from speeding tickets and accident cases to wills and divorces. Lengthy visits to stuffy lawyers' offices and the plush legal bills that accompany them, will become relics of the past, as sophisticated data-gathering and videoconferencing technologies enable service-oriented attorneys to provide quick, comprehensive, personal, and easy-to-understand counsel to Americans who might not otherwise consider seeking a lawyer's help. Longer term, I will build on my business's success to become an advocate, in collaboration with municipal judicial systems, for leveraging technology to create virtual courtrooms where less complex legal matters can be adjudicated efficiently. The time and cost benefits to consumers and the judicial system alike could be enormous.

Why Our School?

■ I believe that earning my J.D. at Berkeley's Boalt Hall School of Law will enable me to develop the intellectual rigor I will need to gain an in-house counsel position with the African office of an environmentally focused nongovernmental organization like Greenpeace or World Wildlife Fund. Boalt's highly regarded concentrations in environmental law and international and comparative legal studies include unique courses such as "Environment and Culture" and "International Environmental Law" that will enable me to use my legal training to interpret and apply international treaties in culturally and economically diverse situations. As a member of Boalt's Environmental Law Society I look forward to using my contacts in the Bay Area's environmental community to recruit speakers for the speaker series, and I hope to be considered for an editorial position with *Ecology Law Quarterly.*

- My decision to pursue law at Northwestern is based on personal observation, my research into the Northwestern law program, and conversations with its students. Above all, I believe that Northwestern School of Law is the ideal program to prepare me for a career of service as an advocate for the medically underserved. Because of its unique interdisciplinary approach, the health law concentration will give me a thorough legal and business foundation in health law. Both Professor Orenstein's research interests and his electives, "Health-Care Delivery Systems" and "Health-Care Law," speak directly to my intellectual and professional interests, and studying with him would be a highlight of my law school years. I also hope to take advantage of the flexibility Northwestern gives students in developing their own externships by creating an individualized program involving work with both attorneys and professionals in the health-care industry. More generally, I admire Northwestern's law student-to-faculty ratio and proximity to the opportunities to promote health-care reform that a major city like Chicago offers.

- Whether I finally decide on dispute resolution or pursue public service law, the ideal program for me is the University of Houston Law Center. The A.A. White

Dispute Resolution Center, part of the Blakely Advocacy Institute, will enable me to gain intensive training in commercial arbitration and family mediation, and A.A. White director Ben Sheppard's courses— "International Litigation and Arbitration" and "International Commercial Arbitration"—will enable me to understand dispute resolution principles outside the United States. During my campus visit in May, Nick Lemecki (J.D., 2009) enthused about Professors Alderman and Ventura's "Consumer Dispute Resolution" course, and introduced me to members of the Christian Legal Society and the International Law Society, two student organizations in which I will pursue leadership roles.

- Whether I ultimately return to the "last stage" of the criminal justice system or seek a public policy-influencing role, a law degree from Hastings College of Law will give me the broadest, most rigorous training in the most diverse learning environment possible. Hastings's Criminal Justice Experiential Program and in-house clinic will provide me with hard lawyering skills while enabling me to continue the work rehabilitating criminals that I began at Second Chapter Halfway House. Similarly, Hastings's Group Representation Course will allow me to extend the counseling work I did with state prison convicts for the Colorado Institute. In short, to become the kind of "bilingual" leader who speaks the language of both the criminal justice system's "enforcers" and its policy makers, I need a program with the rigor, depth, and quality of Hastings College of Law.

- To do so, I need a law school that has programs renowned for their quality, the resources to study women's rights and the law, and, finally, an international focus. The University of Minnesota more than fulfills those requirements. Seminars like "Women's International Human Rights" and the journal *Law and Inequality* will enable me to work with people who share my commitment to exploring inequality and gender issues. The Law and Violence Against Women Clinic, the Domestic Violence Clinic, and the civil rights moot court will give me valuable practical skills I can begin applying immediately in my career. Finally, faculty members like Beverly Balos, who teaches "Law and Violence against Women," and David Weissbrodt, an expert in international and human rights law, will provide the international and women's rights focus my law school of choice must have.

- I'll admit that my interest in UCLA Law was initially inspired by its outstanding national reputation and its location in one of the nation's largest litigation centers and legal job markets. But my conviction that UCLA is the best law program for me came only after Professor Detweiler personally recommended it to me and I discovered the breadth of UCLA's clinical programs and the opportunities it offers to explore every type of law. Several of the attorneys I worked with at Madsen & Kent told me candidly that they did not believe their law schools prepared them adequately to practice law. So it was a relief for me to discover a UCLA clinical education course that uses volunteers as witnesses to emulate the way attorneys must act with "real" clients. My conviction grew when a friend of my brother's, a UCLA Law J.D. (class of 2000), explained that UCLA's emphasis on public interest law can be found not only in its multiple lectures and seminars but in its Public Interest Law Foundation, which grants awards to students who do public interest volunteering. By the time I learned that UCLA Law's clinical program offers the unique opportunity to serve as a judge's law extern—a great way to understand how judicial decisions are made and perhaps even participate in them—I knew where I belonged.

■ Penn Law is my first choice for law school because of the rich opportunities it offers for interdisciplinary study; the warmth and enthusiastic comments of the Penn Law students I've spoken to; and Penn Law's outstanding success at placing J.D.s in law firms with major IP practices. First, the strength of Pennsylvania's intellectual property law program and the larger university's reputation in medicine and technology development make it the ideal place for someone with my biotech IP goals. Penn Law's pioneering courses and seminars in intellectual property law and biomedical development will give me the in-depth knowledge and special skills in patent and trademarks laws I will need as a practicing attorney. Second, Penn Law's number-three satisfaction ranking in a recent survey of summer associates echoed the undiluted praise I've heard from Beth Nicholas (J.D., 2002), Angie Matsuda (J.D., 1997), and Kfir Mermelstein (J.D., 2000)—colleagues of mine at Avogan Pharmaceuticals. They all said that Penn Law's smaller class size and collegial culture made a huge difference in their law school experience. Finally, placement: I was impressed to learn that Penn Law successfully places almost half its J.D.s in the states of New York and California, my home state and the state I hope to practice in, respectively. I know without hesitation or exaggeration that Penn Law is both intellectually and personally the program for me.

- Stanford Law will give me a superlative foundation in legal analysis, research, and writing. Its professional skills courses, such as the Advocacy Skills Workshop, are both attractive to me and relevant to my interests. Finally, I am eager to explore the legal issues that lie at the intersection of law and psychology with Drs. Ankler and Zellman, both trailblazers in the behavioral law and economics field. The small size of Stanford's joint program in psychology and law and its impressive concentration of faculty interested in forensic psychology will give me opportunities literally unmatched by any other program. Yet, if I had to name only one reason for choosing Stanford Law, it would be the people—America's best and brightest. Among them, I hope to find future colleagues, partners, and volunteers. With them, I know I will experience the ultimate challenge: surviving and thriving through three intense years that will transform not just my intellectual and professional skills but my life.

■ I want to earn my J.D. at Fordham University School of Law because I want to learn how U.S. companies are established and how they function within the domestic and international systems. Because of my interest in tax law, I want to focus my second- and third-year course work on federal income tax law, international investments, international business transactions, trade, and bankruptcy law. For Dr. Nathan Gilbert's international investment law class, I hope to analyze the impact of the 2007–2008 credit crisis on India's economy and the reforms needed in Indian business law to stimulate further foreign direct investment. But I'm certain that Dr. Shelly Lund's federal income tax course will also be an exciting learning experience that is unavailable at any other law program.

Chapter 10 Perfect Phrases
for Conclusions

An effective conclusion can do several things all at once. It will offer a wise, amusing, or self-knowing lesson from your essay's stories in an unhackneyed, forward-looking way that seems organic to and yet an enhancement of what's come before. It will give the essay a sense of formal closure that communicates your command of the language (English) the law will insist you master. And it may (though need not) show how the experiences you've focused on in the personal statement connect to your decision to go to law school. Let's consider some perfect phrases for essay conclusions.

■ Sitting on the Kellermans' porch in the cool spring air of eastern Ohio, I realized that my experiences had given me a rare opportunity to peer into the key forces driving the evolution of America's economy. By helping me bridge the two interdependent but often needlessly opposing axes of business practicality and social justice, an education in law and management can help me find the elusive but surely achievable balance between globalization and a just society's social compact.

- My seven-month odyssey taught me how to do construction estimating and scheduling and helped me understand construction contracts and local zoning ordinances. Moreover, I was able to interact with subcontractors, engineers, architects, building owners, and municipal officials—the dramatis personae of the industry. Dealing personally with all these individuals showed me what they were like, what their jobs demanded, and how they responded to the inevitable changes and problems. I view this apprenticeship as not only a foundation but a prerequisite for my future career as a real estate lawyer—a colloquium on the art and science of the real estate trade. I'm now ready for the next stage in that education.

- Working for a nonprofit organization gave me my first opportunity to devise creative ideas that benefited not only an entire organization but the larger community. Implementing my ideas through MetroOrganic's 60 volunteers also strengthened my leadership skills, since the volunteers did not have to do what I asked them to. As a result, today I am less reticent about innovative and assertive strategies even when the risks they pose are significant. Solving existing problems and preempting potential ones, I have learned, is possible only with a proactive, prepared mind.

- For the past three years I have performed intellectual property adjudication work that is traditionally assigned to attorneys. I have learned and successfully performed virtually every phase of the prosecuting patent attorney's role. Combined with my extensive background in the semiconductor engineering industry and my master's degree in electrical engineering, my experience at the Patent and Trademark Office has convinced me that I have the skills and experience required to succeed as an intellectual property attorney. I look forward to beginning that journey at the George Washington University Law School.

- I recognized that I didn't have to be working in an inner-city clinic in Karachi to make a difference. My ability to understand PIKO's goals and convey them to my team so we could produce a blog that delivered PIKO's message showed me that I have a role to play as a conduit between business and nongovernmental organizations. As I reflect on the PIKO project, I have come to realize that partnerships between business and socially minded organizations may actually be the best way to effect social change. Each sector has different strengths, and the combination of resources and abilities can be a powerful vehicle for good works. I will share this insight with my Duke Law classmates.

- Starting An Die Musik was not only my "greatest achievement" but the biggest thrill of my life because it gave me the chance to be a "super fan" of these great masters. Not just limiting myself to autographs, I was actually able to talk to them—"gods" like Leon Fleisher, Gil Shaham, Midori—about their music. It will always be one of the biggest honors of my life. But it was also my first real leadership experience. I learned that there is no substitute for personal dedication and diligence and that thinking big and raising the bar can produce big results. In the end, probably the most gratifying thing about An Die Musik was what made it valuable for others: seeing young students develop, for the first time, a sense of the richness and glory of classical music. A law degree in entertainment law will empower me to spread that message to the world.

■ Turning around my sister's life is easily my greatest achievement. My active intervention, with support from my family, friends, and doctors, saved Erica. Years of coaxing her have taught me the art and value of gentle persuasion, even in the face of irrational suspicion and disbelief. Caring for Erica while juggling my career and my own family has been one of the most difficult challenges of my life and almost cost me my marriage. As a result, I have matured considerably and learned to be patient and persistent in the face of great obstacles. While I used to be very independent, I have learned that some problems can't be tackled alone. I joined a support group to learn coping strategies and mobilized friends and neighbors to help Erica when I had to travel for business. Most importantly, this experience has given me a deep appreciation for the gift of mental health and a profound empathy for sufferers of depression. So much so that I want to build a new career as their legal advocate.

- The challenge and controversy of Bell Industries' IRS audit was truly a "crucible" experience for me because it was the first time I had ever been challenged every step of the way. The audit reinforced my conviction that objective evidence cannot be refuted—and should not be backed away from. It also affirmed that, no matter how bad the odds may sometimes look, two parties can come to agreement once they truly understand all the issues.

- When I entered the family waiting lounge, Frederique's mother hugged me so hard she nearly knocked me over. In that one embrace, my long years of studying, sleep deprivation, and nights on call suddenly fell into perspective. At 11 p.m. on a Saturday night, when most people are enjoying their weekend, studying biochemical pathways and arcane tidbits of pathology can seem an odd use of one's time. Frederique's mother crystallized for me why I had gone to medical school: I wanted to make a contribution to other lives. Her hug told me I had. Today, that same motivation drives my application to Boalt Hall.

- My experience at Cantabile Studios has had a profound influence on my professional development. I learned how to grow a small business and keep it growing, how to recruit and retain top-notch employees, how to manage the financial and "cultural" aspects of a merger, how to juggle the complexities of contracts and documentation, and how to learn from mistakes. I also learned that giving up ground is never as glorious as leading a charge, but that leaders need to do both, and that being honest about retreating is better than selling the retreat as a win. Finally, I learned that leadership isn't always about being the manager with the most visibility, largest staff, or biggest title. Sometimes it's about quietly driving change and efficiently revising perceptions. By leaving an established firm for the uncertain future of a film production start-up I took a calculated risk, but the decision paid off.

- I will never regret becoming a priest. It exposed me to leadership opportunities most 19-year-olds never face. It also gave me the chance to discover what I really want by exploring the alternatives. Deciding to leave the priesthood meant abandoning a life and a definition of myself that had great meaning for me. But because of the sense of challenge and excitement I feel every morning and the positive good my legal career has made possible, I can honestly say it was a decision I have never regretted.

- As my plane descended into John Wayne Airport, I had already won. My decision to embrace change optimistically made it possible for me to land my first job within days of arriving, which set the stage for my next move up, to Pacific Life, a year later. Three months after arriving in Orange County I sold the return portion of my round-trip ticket back home. There was no point in keeping it. My new life in California was well underway, and the last thing I needed was a security blanket.

- This experience taught me that anyone and everyone can suffer from discrimination, despite the laws prohibiting it. I am particularly sensitive now to the stereotypes women face in the oceanic sciences. In college, I noticed that in engineering courses women team members were usually assigned the least technically challenging tasks, for example, literature searches instead of actual design. So in my own senior project, I made sure that this was not the case by dividing the work fairly so everyone was challenged. Professionally, I continue my awareness of discrimination and work to ensure that each of the three women on my Deepwater Sciences team can contribute fully to the team.

- Although Angel Partners has not yet succeeded financially, it has helped me learn what success and consequently failure really mean to me. There is no failure worse than letting down people who put trust in

137

your leadership. Every growth plan I develop in the future will contain a detailed contingency plan that will allow me to minimize, if not eliminate, the need to downsize. I have learned that success is not only about the success of a product or financial gain; it must also include the success of every contributor.

- I had naively believed that decisions involving the environment were primarily driven by facts and not political considerations. I quickly learned that, in contrast to the predictable world of engineering science, even solutions with a clear quantitative and logical basis can be sacrificed in favor of short-term political benefits. Reevaluating my faith in the effectiveness of rational decision making was not easy. But today I understand how to take political influences into account when making fact-driven decisions. It's to magnify the scope of that understanding that I seek a law degree from Washington University.

- Whenever I recall that morning in Fallujah, I sit up straight and thank God for getting me out of there. I also thank the bus driver who mustered the courage to drive past the mob. Surprisingly, he was from the same tribe as the rioters and didn't support the imposition of Shiite rule any more than they did. Unlike them, he chose to protect us even at the risk of his own life. The bridge he built that day saved our lives and reinforced my belief that, in spite of cultural and geographical distances, we still share the common bonds of humanity.

■ This experience made me realize that leadership is more than increasing the return on your investment; sometimes it's just a matter of keeping your word. I also discovered that working to make environments fulfilling for others is an outstanding way to make them fulfilling for yourself. Finally, I learned that my effective leadership "modes" can include organizing, evangelizing, and a small bit of nagging. Though I never thought of myself as a fund-raiser, I see now that I have two of the key traits—the ability to be nice and demanding at the same time.

■ Although my memories of Rick's abuse have been packed away along with my ballet shoes, pageant trophies, and cheerleading pom-poms, I have used the experience to guide my career focus toward the intersection of law and psychology. I'm eagerly anticipating a fascinating and accomplished professional career and look forward to the opportunity to prepare for that career at Gould School of Law.

■ I learned many lessons from Dr. Nussman's class besides how to "excavate" biblical texts. I learned what it means to be passionate about ideas, how to closely analyze texts, and how to grow by challenging yourself to do more than you thought you could. I also learned that real wisdom does indeed exist and that speaking charismatically and speaking profoundly do not necessarily go hand in hand. At Groton, at Yale, and on Capitol Hill I met innumerable smart people, and I will meet many more in law school. But I've been in the presence of genius only once; fortunately, that was enough to change my life.

- Seeing the determined faces of these children has helped me to understand the concept of teamwork in new ways. Disabled, I have learned, does not mean "unabled"—my kids' ability to work together as a team is as natural and sincere as any "normal" group of people I've ever met. Founding DisabledCan.org has not enabled me to realize my dream of eliminating prejudice against the physically challenged, but it has enabled me to sow the seeds of that transformation.

Part III

Chapter 11 Perfect Phrases for Addenda and Other Application Documents

"Additional Information. We encourage you to provide any relevant information that may be helpful to us in making an informed decision on your application. Any information that you believe to be relevant to your application is appropriate. Examples of information that may be relevant to individual cases include unusual circumstances that may have affected academic performance, a description or documentation of a physical or learning disability, an explicit history of standardized test results, or a history of educational or sociological disadvantage."

(Harvard)

"If you answer yes to any of the questions, you must provide a supplementary statement including details, the current status of any disciplinary action or judicial sanctions, and the final resolution of the issues involved."

(Duke)

Though some law schools will invite you to discuss extenuating circumstances like poor LSAT scores or grades in optional essays, it's better to do your damage control in addenda, that is, short supplementary statements submitted in addition to your personal statement and secondary essays (whether required or optional). By using addenda, you free up valuable essay space for positive material like achievements or diversity experiences.

Addenda should be short, fact-driven, objective in tone, and honest. Explain what happened in enough detail to satisfy the admission reader's doubts and then mention any positive, exculpatory facts that may mitigate the circumstance you're trying to explain, for example, the efforts you've made to demonstrate your intellectual preparedness since failing three classes your freshman year. This chapter provides perfect phrases for common addenda topics: grades and LSAT scores, work-related circumstances, choice of recommenders, and what you've done since your first application to law school.

Where addenda are optional statements that you may or may not decide you need to submit, conduct statements are nondiscretionary. If you answer yes to a school's "character and fitness" questions—usually about academic suspensions, crime-related arrests or convictions, military discharges, or previous law school enrollments—you *must* explain what happened. We've included some representative perfect phrases for conduct statements in this chapter.

We close it with some perfect phrases for four other common application documents: transfer essays, application essays for LLM programs, letters of recommendation, and wait-list letters.

Addenda

Addenda on LSAT and Academic Performance

- I believe the professional success I've enjoyed both as an engineer in the flat-panel display industry and as a patent examiner for the U.S. government demonstrates that I have the intellectual skills to thrive in law school. In this respect, I believe my undergraduate record at Case Western Reserve is an anomaly that bears explaining. In the fall of my freshman year at Case Western, both my parents were killed in a car accident on their way home from church services. As I am an only child and was especially close to both my parents, this was a devastating emotional blow for me that immediately affected my academic focus and my grades. Moreover, the loss of my parents' financial support shifted the burden of funding my education onto me, and working a 30-hour a week job at Great Lakes Labs intensified my academic challenge. Learning to overcome these obstacles—which I believe my junior- and senior-year grades show I did— strengthened my determination to live up to my parents' memory and fulfill my highest potential. My academic performance in the electrical engineering master's program at University of Maryland, my LSAT score, and the success I have enjoyed at Sharp and the

Patent and Trademark Office are evidence that I am doing that. In the nine years since I lost my parents, I believe I have built a record that shows I am the kind of exceptional law school applicant whom raw numbers alone cannot define. I respectfully ask the admissions committee to place my undergraduate academic performance in this broader context.

- I would like to clarify for the Admissions Committee the discrepancy between the cumulative GPA of 3.32 stated on my Law School Data Assembly Service Law School Report and the GPA of 3.43 indicated on my official transcript from George Mason University. The difference is completely explained by the LSDAS's selective conversion of the grades of "satisfactory" and "unsatisfactory" I earned in three courses between my sophomore and senior years. As a matter of publicly stated policy, George Mason has never and does not now count "satisfactory" and "unsatisfactory" grades when determining a student's GPA. For reasons that are unclear to me, however, LSDAS converted my grade of "unsatisfactory" in my German Lab III and counted it against my cumulative GPA, but did not so convert my "satisfactory" grades in German Labs I and II. I have written to LSDAS explaining this error and have attached my letter to this addendum.

- I respectfully ask the committee to note that once I entered college, it was always my intention to fully

engage myself extracurricularly. Thus, in addition to
my full course load during my four years at Bryn Mawr,
I was active in three student organizations (student
senate, volleyball, and the student newspaper) and
averaged 20 hours per week in my part-time job. Much
of the time I could have spent chasing A's was devoted
to fulfilling leadership responsibilities in my
extracurricular commitments and working to pay for
nearly half of my private-university education. In this
context, I believe my GPA of 3.19 in an academically
rigorous college is commendable. I therefore ask the
admissions committee to regard my LSAT score of 168
rather than my GPA as the best predictor of my ability
to thrive at Vanderbilt Law.

■ In the equity research business it's often said that "the
case for a company is made on the income statement,
but the verdict is rendered by the balance sheet."
Similarly, in the law school admissions business you are
asked to appraise a candidate's "forward value" by
evaluating both a historical record of performance
(namely, grades and professional success) that is much
like an income statement and a static snapshot (the
LSAT score) that resembles the corporate balance sheet.
In appraising my income statement and balance sheet,
you must decide whether I am an entity worth
investing in, and the inconsistency between my
undergraduate transcript and my LSAT score may cause

➡

you hesitation. In the spring semester of my sophomore year at Dartmouth my father was unexpectedly diagnosed with a malignant brain tumor that completely debilitated him within a year and killed him within two. My father's illness ripped my family apart and created emotional and financial insecurity that I had not the slightest idea how to handle. As much as I loved my economics classes, I was distracted and depressed and repeatedly missed exams or failed to complete papers. Nothing I tried over the next two years—withdrawing from school to earn an income, changing majors, or seeking professional help—helped. When my father finally passed away in the spring of what would have been my senior year, I began to find closure and pull myself together. My grades in my final year of classes rose from a 2.3 average to a 3.8 average, and I was fortunate to find a rewarding and challenging position with the Congressional Budget Office. When the experiences I describe in my personal statement made clear to me that my future lay in the law, I took the LSAT. I believe the 172 score I earned demonstrates my ability to succeed in law school. Because I am certain that a career as a lobbyist is my true calling, I ask the committee to understand the context of my undergraduate record.

- I was diagnosed with moderate dyslexia by Dr. Timothy Adler of the Peoria Children's Clinic when I was nine years old (see enclosed document). Because of my condition, for every hour my classmates spent reading class assignments, it usually took me two to three hours. For this reason, when I took the SAT, GRE, and LSAT, I was granted twice the usual time. Though I scored a 161 on the LSAT, I struggled with the reading comprehension section and was able to complete only 21 of the 24 analytical reasoning questions. However, I answered every single one of those 21 questions correctly. I believe this suggests that I would have achieved a much higher score had my dyslexia not prevented me from completing the entire analytical reasoning section. I ask the admissions committee to take my dyslexia into account when evaluating my LSAT score.

- While I make no excuses for my mediocre academic performance at Goucher, I believe the committee should understand the concrete reasons why my GPA is not indicative of my ability to succeed at USC Gould. Growing up with an abusive father affected my self-esteem in ways I am still coming to grips with. Lacking any reassurance or positive role models at home, I was fearful about approaching high school teachers with even simple questions. My self-isolation prevented me from developing any mentoring relationships with adults, and hence my potential remained untapped. These obstacles were amplified by a childhood spent in a rural town in one of Maryland's poorest counties. I never lacked ambition, but I had no idea what it took to succeed. Then in May 2003, two weeks before Goucher's spring-term finals, I was sexually assaulted by a classmate. After a brief but necessary stay in the emergency room, I spent a week in campus health services recovering. My medical injuries, though serious, were minor compared to my emotional and psychic trauma, which reopened the childhood psychological wounds I had just begun to come to terms with.

■ Should my disappointing GPA raise concerns about my academic aptitude? I don't believe so. As my transcript shows, in summer 2000 I participated in a high school program that enabled me to take three UCLA courses, in which I earned a 4.0 GPA. As a college student at UCLA, in semesters when I was not distracted by my duties as starting wide receiver for the Bruins, I maintained a 3.42 average in a course load that included calculus and engineering classes. Moreover, up to my senior year, my transcripts show an upward trend in performance, especially as I entered my area of concentration. I believe the full context of my academic performance demonstrates that I am more than prepared to handle the academic challenges that George Washington University offers me.

- My undergraduate grades do not reflect my ability to handle University of Wisconsin Law School's rigorous curriculum. They are primarily the result of the impact my mother's battle with kidney disease had on me in my last year and half at Beloit College. As the only child, my father needed my help in caring for her. I took leaves of 7–10 days about 10 times during that period, not counting summer vacations, to travel the 575 miles to and from Thunder Bay. My grades and project work suffered as a result. Throughout this emotionally exhausting period, my priority was my family, and my main academic objective was just to complete my degree requirements on schedule—which I did—so that I could spend time at home. This was the sole reason my academic performance fell below my dean's list performance in my first three years. It has been more than eight years since I graduated from college. As my résumé amply demonstrates, I have matured both professionally and personally. My success on the LSAT and in a complex and rigorous profession, not grades in courses I took a decade ago, should constitute, I believe, the primary desideratum in determining my potential for academic success at Stanford. I have demonstrated a consistent record of achievement and communicative skill that greatly minimizes the significance of my undergraduate transcript.

■ With respect to my LSAT score, I would like to emphasize to the committee that although English is a second language for me, it is one I have completely mastered, both orally and in written form. Today I routinely research, write, and present consulting proposals and reports, externally for Advanced Informatics' clients and internally for our management and business development group. Last year I was honored to submit a white paper on informatics trends for an industry conference sponsored by Advanced Informatics. It was nominated for a prestigious Best Practices Award. Finally, Advanced Informatics would never have placed me in charge of more than 10 client-facing auditing engagements annually if it had any concerns about my verbal skills. I am confident in my ability to analyze, write, and speak English like a native speaker and believe that the evidence should inspire this same confidence in the admissions committee.

Addenda on Professional-Related Issues

■ I would like to explain the three-month gap in my work history, from January 2007 to April 2007. When San Diego's residential real estate market began to implode, mortgages services companies like my employer, Pacific Escrow, were the first to bear the brunt. Shortly after

Christmas 2006, I was notified that my escrow support group was being eliminated, despite our award-winning work over the preceding three years. I was devastated, but I immediately began seeking a new position. Unfortunately, the Southern California housing market continued to worsen, and I was unable to find a job until April, when I joined Balboa Debt Collection Services as a compliance manager. Throughout my three months of full-time job searching, I continued to volunteer weekly as an English tutor at my church, began and completed a legal issues course at Poway Community College, and helped my husband open a new surfing supplies shop in suburban San Diego. I believe the reasons for my brief unemployment and the activities I pursued during it reflect positively on me and my potential for success at Loyola Law School.

- A minuscule fraction of all medical school students—less than 1 percent—do not graduate. Most who leave do so, like me, for deeply personal reasons and no doubt find their decision one of the hardest they have ever faced. I would like to explain in this addendum why I made the difficult decision to leave medical school three years ago. That decision grew out of my answer to the question my first clinical experiences posed to me: What kind of life would I be leading if every patient's death or incurable diagnosis left me feeling a sense of failure and despair? I hadn't even thought to ask that question until my second-year Skills and Science of Doctoring clinical module.

- I would like to explain more fully why I decided to leave Bearing Point to join Potomac Partners Consultants and why that transition was a protracted one. My year and a half at Bearing Point was a valuable learning experience for me, but by early 2007 the learning and challenge were beginning to decelerate. More importantly, after my experience in the 2006 Republican campaign, described in my personal statement, I knew that a strategy consulting job would never be as rewarding for me as political consulting. Unfortunately, I let this realization influence the enthusiasm I brought to my daily work, for in October 2007 I became one of five consultants downsized when Bearing Point's banking practice slowed. Though at that point I had already begun networking my way toward a position with a political consulting firm, it took me another three months to find the right fit—with Potomac Partners Consultants.

- In 2006, I was hired for an entry-level editorial role at Graeble Publications, a small hobbyists' magazine publisher in Reno, Nevada. As associate section editor, I was responsible for the substantive and copyediting of the features sections of three Graeble publications: *DIY Furniture Making, DIY Home Maintenance,* and *DIY Auto Repair.* Because I had served as the editor in chief

of Brigham Young's student newspaper I believed
I brought some degree of editorial skill to my new
duties. Within weeks of my start, however, my editorial
director and I were disagreeing over the quality of my
work. She repeatedly questioned my substantive or
developmental advice to authors but also my specific
copyediting decisions, from word choice matters to
grammatical mechanics like agreement. I was always
willing to defend and explain my edits and even cited
the editorial authorities, like Strunk & White and the
Chicago Manual of Style, that Graeble's house style
conformed to. She rarely accepted my explanations,
however, and left me with the impression that I had
deceived her about my editorial skill (though she
herself had graded my initial copyediting test). Within
two months of joining Graeble, I was let go. Though
I remain convinced that the quality of my work was not
the reason for my dismissal, I was relieved to be free of
a workplace environment that had become untenable.
I immediately found a new position with *Las Vegas*
magazine, where I quickly rose to assistant senior
editor.

■ I would like to explain to the committee why I left
JeoVision after only six months. Before joining the
company full time in May 2006, I had worked as an IT
contractor for six months in its sales and marketing
department. Because I was looking for ways to break

into technical sales, I loved the environment and the department. My client manager knew of my sales/marketing interest and went out of his way to expose me to sales functions. When a full-time opening came up for a technical liaison with JeoVision's development department that April, the sales and marketing client manager suggested I take it and promised me it was really a "stepping stone" position into a direct technical sales position. Though that would have been just what I wanted, it did not turn out to be the case. In fact, the full-time position took me even further from JeoVision's sales/marketing functions and turned out to be a straight technical role. When Oracle offered me a true technical sales position—exactly what I had been looking for—that November I decided to jump at the chance. It was a difficult experience for me, and I know that I should have done more due diligence rather than relying on the client manager's assurances about the nature of the job. I learned a lot about doing my "homework" and taking responsibility for my actions.

Addenda on Choice of Recommenders

- I have not asked my current supervisor at Sunoco to submit a recommendation on my behalf because I have been with the firm for only three months. My supervisor is quite pleased with my work, but my projects have not advanced sufficiently for him to comment meaningfully on my performance. Moreover, my prelaw professor at the University of Texas and my supervisor at Marathon Oil have worked with me much more closely on multiple projects over many months. Thus, they are in a much better position to comment authoritatively on my performance and potential.

- Although Dr. Lewis Zagbi was the advisor for my bachelor's thesis and I studied under him in three classes, I have decided not to ask him for a recommendation letter. I earned A's in his classes and received honors for my thesis, but after my thesis work had been approved Dr. Zagbi and I had a falling out after the breakup of my relationship with his daughter, Emma, whom I met at a student mixer at Dr. Zagbi's home in my junior year. My decision to end my relationship with Emma stemmed from both personal and professional factors, but I admit I handled it poorly and that Emma took it badly. Dr. Zagbi was understandably disappointed in me, but he wished me well professionally. Because I value his goodwill and honor the opportunity he gave me to work with him, I want to avoid burdening him with an obligation that he may feel uncomfortable fulfilling. Moreover, I took two courses (including one independent study) with Dr. Miles Caudill, who was also the faculty advisor for

the Philology Club I cofounded in my junior year.
I believe Dr. Caudill can provide the committee with all
the insights it requires into my undergraduate
academic and leadership abilities.

Addenda on Reapplication

- Reapplying to New York University School of Law is not
  a decision I take lightly. This past spring, I was accepted
  at two excellent J.D. programs. I made the difficult
  decision to turn down their offers and reapply to NYU
  for two reasons. The first is that my father's diabetes
  worsened this past spring and led to his temporary
  hospitalization. Since neither of my brothers was in a
  position to help support my immigrant parents through
  my father's medical crisis, I delayed school and focused
  both my financial and emotional resources on
  supporting my family. The second reason is that I
  continue to believe that NYU's J.D. program is the best
  one for me and that I should not settle for anything less.

- Being wait-listed by the University of Virginia in June
  gave me several months in which to reflect on what
  I really want out of law school. As I was doing so, my
  alma mater, St. Xavier High, invited me back to speak to
  students about my experiences at Clemson and as a
  paralegal with Draughton & Speakes. As I stood before
  those three hundred souls—exhorting them to find a

college and a profession they truly love—I realized that obtaining the best legal education I can and becoming the kind of lawyer my father would respect are much too important to compromise by earning my J.D. at a law school that I learned too late does not offer the resources I need. That is why I decided to decline the offer of the law school that accepted me and to reapply at the University of Virginia. Since that first application, I believe I have taken the steps to prove to the admissions committee that I deserve to earn my J.D. where my father earned his.

- In the months since my first application to Emory Law I have gained valuable full-time work experience at the National Park Service's Kennesaw Mountain National Battlefield Park as a researcher and Civil War guide. I also obtained my real estate agent's license, which I will begin to use in late January. Above all, my experiences over the past year have only confirmed my belief that the law is what I wish to devote my career and life to. I reapply to Emory University's School of Law today with deepened experience, renewed optimism, and an LSAT score four points higher than the one I submitted last year.

- Delaying law school has enabled me to continue to refine my leadership and professional skills. In September, I received the highest possible performance evaluation for a counselor (a 10 rating on a scale of 10), and the Public Support Agency has asked me to undertake a strategic review of its adult counseling services, working directly with director of adult counseling, Marianne Wu. Of course, I also continue to provide counseling myself, and since June have taken on five new mental health clients. As I searched myself to be sure reapplying to Notre Dame was really the best course for me, I sought out NDLS alumni for insight. Nick Kotovic (J.D., 2001) told me that Notre Dame's GALILEE (Group Alternative Live-in Legal Education Experience) would give me excellent opportunities to apply my counseling experience in a legal context by learning the legal needs of the poor in a major U.S. inner city. And Hsien Lee (J.D., 2008) enthused that Professor Kent Hall's "Law of the Disabled" was a one-of-a-kind learning experience for him. He assured me that Notre Dame's professors are "really accessible and very dedicated teachers, committed to making sure we get the most out of law school." The new insights I've gained into Notre Dame Law have convinced me to reapply to my first-choice school. Notre Dame Law School is the one school worth waiting for.

Conduct Statements

■ As a freshman at Oral Roberts University in 2001, a friend unaffiliated with the university asked me to go to the pharmacy to get him some cold medicine, as he was feeling ill. I agreed, and while taking a shortcut

I knew through ORU's campus, was stopped by a university security squad car for going six miles faster than the posted speed limit. The security officer asked to see my driver's license and student ID and then wanted to know whether I'd ingested any alcohol. In keeping with the university's honor code that "I will not lie," I told him truthfully that I had not, and when he asked me if there was any alcohol in the car, I answered truthfully that there was—a six-pack of Budweiser I had seen my friend purchase and place there that morning. Since I was a 19-year-old minor, the officer informed me that he had the legal authority to search my friend's vehicle. They found the beer and promptly took me to the campus security headquarters. The officer there told me that because I had been honest with him and the alcohol had been in the car's trunk and not the cab, they would not notify the Tulsa police. However, he said they were duty bound to notify the university. Because I was technically "in possession of" of intoxicants though I had not violated the university's proscription against drinking alcohol, the university placed a disciplinary sanction in my file, but began no more serious disciplinary process against me. I regret the incident, but believe it does not reflect negatively on my moral fitness to practice the law.

- On October 3, 2007, I was ticketed for a "Minor in Possession of Alcohol" citation while participating at a Clemson football pregame party at my fraternity house. We had been in the house's parking lot grilling hamburgers and sipping beers when police officers responded to a loud music complaint. Seven minor-in-possession tickets were subsequently handed out. While I greatly regret violating an ordinance that I believe is both necessary and just, this incident was an aberration from my normal conduct. I have had alcohol on only three occasions in my life, serve as Boy Scout troop leader, and in 2003 was named a Teen Role Model by my church. On November 1, 2007, the Pickens County Court granted my request for deferred adjudication. I attended an alcohol awareness class a week later and performed eight hours of community service by the end of November. I'm happy to have put this incident behind me, and I look forward to applying my ethical principles to a career of service as a practicing attorney in the great state of South Carolina.

■ On September 6, 2002, I was arrested in Davis County for soliciting a prostitute. I had no prior criminal record, adjudication was withheld, and the record has been legally sealed. I want to assure the admissions committee that quite aside from the legal consequences and perhaps professional consequences of my mistake, the events of that night will stay with me for the rest of my life. Because of it, I lost not only my self-respect, but a relationship I cared deeply about and several thousand dollars in court costs and attorney fees. It has left an indelible psychic scar that I still deal with today. Above all, it has sensitized me to the circumstances of the accused I hope to one day help, as I know better than most the consequences that one moment's mistake can have on a life that is otherwise free of even the slightest ethical blemish. It was an isolated, regrettable incident that will not happen again and one that I believe will actually make me a more effective defender of the law and servant of the accused. I have enclosed a copy of the seal order. I will gladly and forthrightly answer any questions the admissions committee may have about this matter.

- When I was 18 years old, I was arrested for, charged with, and convicted of the possession and use of less than one ounce of nonmedicinal marijuana under Section 16.2 of the city charter of Ann Arbor, Michigan. Though this constituted a civil infraction rather than a misdemeanor or felony, the offense is of relevance to my ability to pass the state of Michigan's rigorous character-and-fitness process for lawyers aspiring to practice in Michigan. I have researched Michigan's character-and-fitness review process and corresponded with Kathy Swendson of the state bar of Michigan's Standing Committee on Character and Fitness. Ms. Swendson gave me material indicating that only about 3 percent of the 1,350 applications seeking approval each year have committed offenses that are considered serious enough to warrant an evidentiary hearing before the committee. A much smaller percentage is ultimately denied. Moreover, in Ms. Swendson's experience those applications that receive denials usually do so because the applicant was not fully candid with the committee, not because of the substantive nature of the acts in question. I regret my youthful offense. However, because I have been and will continue to be absolutely forthright regarding the circumstances of my offense, I confidently hope the admissions committee will agree with me that my error of judgment will not be an impediment to winning the opportunity to practice law in Michigan.

Transfer Essays

■ "You would love it here, Anne." Nadine Weiss and I have been "soul mates"—and friendly competitors—since we first met in Professor Agee's Western Social Traditions class our freshman year at Swarthmore. With (eerily) similar interests we wound up taking many of the same classes, selected the same major (social philosophy), and even participated in many of the same extracurricular activities. When we both decided to apply to law school, even our friends told us to "get a life." But Nadine and I actually made our law school decisions for very different reasons. Hoping to pursue a joint J.D./master of arts in Islamic studies, Nadine had aimed for the University of Pennsylvania Law School from the start and was delirious when she was admitted. Inspired by my minor in economics, I hoped for admission to George Mason School of Law, famous for its law and economics emphasis. GMU accepted me, and I've been pleased with the caliber of the students and professors. But from Nadine's first reports from Philadelphia, I sensed that she was experiencing a qualitatively different kind of education. When I visited her early in the semester, I was expecting the realities of the first-year law experience to have softened her zeal. But Nadine was still excited and happy, enthusing about Professor Feldman's torts class and the supportiveness of her section members. I had such a good time at Rittenhouse Farmers Market and during our cruise down the Delaware that I visited Nadine again last October.

I learned more about Penn Law, from the excellence of Professor Catherine Struve and Penn Law "Revue" to the opportunities to earn a certificate at Wharton and become a legal writing instructor for 1L students. If I didn't know and trust Nadine as well as I do, I would be content earning my J.D. at George Mason. But because Nadine and I have always thought so much alike, I know what I've learned and continue to learn about Penn Law are worth trusting—and acting on: I'm excited to seek request transfer admission to the University of Pennsylvania's J.D. program.

■ I was lucky to gain admission to Hofstra University School of Law. Because of my battle with Crohn's disease my sophomore year, my grade point average was below Hofstra's middle 50 percent range, and my LSAT was below the median. I was frankly one of those applicants for whom law school is a short-term answer to a long-term question that remained very unclear. The summer before I began at Hofstra, I took a family friend up on his offer to clerk at his environmental law firm in Boulder, Colorado. It may sound clichéd, but those three months were literally a life-changing experience for me. Within days I was helping lawyers at Stansfield Utler escort a major Colorado corporation through the intricacies of state and federal permitting processes so it could expand its manufacturing facility in an area identified by environmentalists as threatened. I was fascinated to learn about the provenance of landmark federal environmental acts like the Clean Water Act and Toxic Substances Control Act and intrigued by the subtle balance the law must strike between the justified interests of businesses seeking to exploit natural resources and environmentalists seeking to protect them. My research into Colorado regulatory law ultimately helped our client prevail in an administrative hearing seeking relief from an overburdensome EPA regulation. I loved my time at Stansfield Utler and in Boulder, and I moved to New York City increasingly certain of why I needed a J.D. I decided to use my first year at Hofstra as a way of ensuring that environmental law was really where my future lies. Being a 1L at Hofstra has been an intense and satisfying experience, but it has only deepened my certainty that environmental law is my "niche." I am applying for transfer to the University of Colorado Boulder because I want to practice in Colorado but primarily because of the rich resources in environmental law that UCB offers, from the Natural Resources Law Center to the Natural Resources Litigation Clinic.

LLM Essays

- As an undergraduate studying history at Dresden University, I attended multiple lectures on the Third Reich and the ideology of the Nazi regime. One of the lectures dealt with the cruel eugenics experiments practiced by Nazi doctors in the concentration camps for the purpose of using genetic selection to "enhance" the "Aryan race." I was horrified by these facts and began focusing my studies on the social, political, and legal implications of biomedical research on human subjects and the application of biotechnology. Although I am convinced that humanity can benefit from modern biotechnology, I am also concerned that such techniques as human cloning and germ line intervention could lead to attempts to "breed" human beings. My major research and now career interest concerns the question of how to legally and ethically apply biotechnology for the benefit of humanity while preventing its abuse. Pursuing an LLM at University of California Berkeley will give me the intellectual foundation and practical skills I will need to begin answering this difficult question.

■ My lifelong commitment to using law to effect positive social change is the direct result of my experiences in Dubai, United Arab Emirates, and Beirut, Lebanon. Although I was born in Beirut, I was raised in Dubai, where my parents chose to reside during the Lebanese civil war of 1975–1990. In contrast to the anarchy that prevailed in my native land, the compassionate sheikdom of the UAE provided its citizens with standards of civil law that preserved individuals' rights and discouraged racial and religious discrimination. The climate of tolerance and law I experienced in the UAE and in my own family instilled in me the conviction that no society can ever become civilized without the diversity of thought that freedom offers because such freedom enables people to think, create, and pursue their hopes and aspirations to the best of their abilities. When I returned to Beirut in 2004, I found my life suddenly transformed from the comfort I had enjoyed in the UAE to the daily challenge of securing adequate water, electricity, and telephone service, all of which were still rationed. I had to learn to find practical solutions to everyday problems, and I was also confronted with my first major life decision. Although by the time of my arrival in Beirut, the Lebanese civil war had long ended, Lebanon is still scarred by the absence of laws and law enforcement agencies. Indeed, the only dominant law was Darwin's survival of the fittest. I was appalled to discover that Lebanon's fragile legal system was being exploited by politicians, government officials, and local chieftains. Corruption was rampant, and laws were fabricated and ignored. For me, the chief question became how to adjust from a life in a civil society to life in a jungle. While the biggest decision many students have to face is what to declare as a major, I was faced with a more fundamental decision: whether to become one of the unethical people I saw all around me or to do everything in my power to change the situation in my native country. Because I am essentially a stranger in my own country, I have decided to seek a legal education that will enable me to return to Lebanon one day and as a practicing attorney convince the Lebanese that only the enforcement of laws enables societies to advance and achieve freedom, harmony, and civil liberty.

- In September 2006, I participated in a convention on intellectual property law and e-commerce sponsored by the International Comparative Law Society in Tokyo. Listening to the presentations, I was struck not only by how differently the Asian and U.S. legal systems treat these issues but also by the lack of uniformity even within the ASEAN nations. The United States still dominates the highly specialized and rapidly developing fields of patents, copyrights, trademarks, and information technology and also represents the frontier for the commercial application of both technologies. To be successful in this highly globalized segment of the legal profession I need rigorous, firsthand study at "the source." I want to earn an LLM in IP and information law so I can position myself to join a globally oriented law firm in Hong Kong or the United States that has international clients in the high-tech and/or media industries.

- The strength of Berkeley's LLM program is evident in the rich variety of its curriculum and in the resources it provides that are relevant to my academic and professional interests. For example, Boalt Hall's Center for Business, Law & Economics is renowned as one of the world's foremost academic institutions for the study of business and law and their social implications. Similarly, in my first semester at Boalt, I can look forward to the course "Analytical Methods for Business, Law and Policy" as well as courses in bankruptcy law. I also hope to take "Comparative Legal History" and "Negotiations:

Theory and Practice," both of which directly relate to my litigation work. In the second semester, I would enroll in "Corporate Finance and Bankruptcy Reorganization" as well as the "Takings Clause" seminar. With the background I gain from these and other courses, I hope to participate in the seminar on corporate bankruptcy as well as the "Jurisprudence of War" seminar (Professor Fletcher). It's a simple fact: few law schools offer as varied and rigorous an LLM program as Boalt Hall.

■ My need for an LLM degree from an American university stems directly from my belief in multidisciplinary perspectives and my desire to improve the teaching of law in Argentina. In July and August of 2005 I gained my first insights into U.S. law and the American style of teaching law during the Georgetown summer program. Seeing the tremendous difference between the U.S. and Argentine styles of teaching law was a revelatory experience for me. Whereas the Argentine style is lecture based, American professors use an exciting blend of class discussion and sophisticated dialogue. Today Argentina's law schools are debating whether to adopt this interactive style, and I have already applied it with great success in my own classes in Córdoba. By studying in an American LLM program I can gain valuable experience in innovative pedagogical techniques for the legal classroom that will have direct benefit in my teaching activities at Universidad Nacional de Córdoba and perhaps throughout my country's educational system.

- I wish to pursue my LLM at the University of Houston because it offers a rigorous program that combines a highly specialized curriculum with both academic and practical education in IP law. No such specialized program in the field of IP law exists today in Southeast Asia, let alone one with the reputation and depth of the University of Houston's. I have chosen the LLM Concentration Program in IP and Information Law rather than the Foreign Scholars Program because through such courses as "International Intellectual Property" and "Computer Law" I can gain intensive instruction in the areas of law I will practice as an attorney in Thailand. Moreover, I expect to gain direct professional and personal benefit from working with U.S. students. The International Law Institute and its conferences, the *Houston Journal of International Law*, and the International Law Society will give me unparalleled access to the leading-edge thought and best minds in global law. The University of Houston's placement resources and reputation are also outstanding, and the diversity of students I will meet there will contribute to an energy and depth of learning that few programs can match. To the University of Houston and my LLM classmates I will offer my extensive experience in the

Thai legal system, my multicultural and language skills (Thai, English, and Chinese), and my firsthand knowledge of the Southeast Asian software and IT industries.

Letters of Recommendation

Introductions

- I'm delighted to have this opportunity to warmly recommend Shanice Matte to you for admission to your J.D. program. She is an exceptionally gifted individual with the analytical and language skills to succeed in law school. I give her my strongest endorsement.

- It is my pleasure to heartily endorse James Nomo's application for admission to Yale Law School. He has a brilliant and creative mind, a genuine and charismatic personality, and the drive and moral vision to achieve an outstanding reputation for himself in the law.

- I am the Bateson Professor Emeritus of History at Arizona State University and chairman of the university's history department. I have taught at the university for over 20 years and served as a prelaw advisor for three years. I teach a historiographic methods class open to undergraduates and graduate-level seminars (open to select undergraduates) in Native American history, problems in North American colonialism, and the history of the Southwest United States.

- After earning my J.D. at Marquette University, I joined the juvenile division of the Milwaukee County Office of the Public Guardian. After being promoted to courtroom supervisor, I began supervising three staff attorneys, two interviewers, and about a dozen law students (clerks). In my 10 years in this position, I've supervised close to 100 law clerks, so in this letter I am comparing Margaret's performance to a large, talented, and relevant pool of peers. In 2008 I was assigned to the estates division of the Public Guardian's office.

- Jason took my Introduction to Epistemology course in 2002 and then my seminars on Kant and Heidegger in 2003. Though his comments and performance in my epistemology course certainly established him as one of my more engaged and capable students, it wasn't until the two seminars in 2003 that I gained a clear picture of the quite remarkable maturity and incisiveness of his mind. When he asked me to be his bachelor's thesis advisor, I was of course happy to comply. During its gestation, Jason sought my counsel frequently, and I came to know him rather well. I am comfortable stating that Jason is one of only a handful of undergraduates I've taught over 25 years whom I am pleased to call a personal friend.

- I hired Anton Rodriguez in 2003 on the strength of his college degree in marketing, the caliber of his undergraduate institution (University of Nebraska), and above all his outstanding interview with me. In contrast to most of the candidates who preceded him, Anton presented me with a polished, articulate, and engaging persona, questions that indicated real knowledge of the industrial meter industry, and a well-defined set of professional goals. For the past two years he has lived up to that initial impression and then some. As my marketing assistant and then associate marketing manager, Anton has been my right-hand man in driving this department's growth from a four-person operation to the largest marketing organization in Dunlop Meter's Midwest region. I have worked side by side with Anton throughout this period and can speak authoritatively about his outstanding sales, presentation, and interpersonal skills; his very solid market research abilities; and his instinctive "solution provider" mindset.

Law-Related Skills and Interests

- Kiara's interest in sustainable development has been obvious to me since she joined the firm. When we launched our environmental services division, she volunteered to put together the marketing package for it, which entailed a significant amount of research into the local environmental service market, relevant city and county codes, and the like. Her finished product was as meaty and knowledgeable as it was visually arresting. Kiara has a real gift for taking the often vaguely expressed ideas of our mostly visually oriented engineers and architects and expressing them in cogent, lucid, "actionable" words. Reflecting her growing interest in environmental law, last June Kiara joined our informal Leadership in Energy and Environmental Design (LEED) study group and has taken online courses through the U.S. Green Building Council to build some environmental expertise on top of her marketing education. In August, Kiara volunteered to draft the detailed descriptions of the development projects and design guidelines that we submit to clients and approving agencies. This required that she research comparable projects, zoning requirements, and general plan requirements and understand the entitlement and approval process of the Army Corps of Engineers, county and city governments, and various environmental groups. Kiara did an outstanding job on this, and all of it was on her own initiative and effort. I was not at all surprised when Kiara told me she was going to earn a J.D. in environmental law. She and I know that she could build a successful career on the development side, but her interests obviously lie with environmental and land-use planning, regulation, and enforcement. She clearly has the intellect, verbal skills, and dedication of the environmental attorneys we work with.

- Deirdre's analysis of Wallace Stevens's "Sunday Morning" was better than most of the papers my graduate-level students give me. Aside from the effort she clearly invested in researching Stevens's life and the poem's extensive critical tradition, Deirdre has a remarkable feel for the connotative breadth and nuance of the English language, as well as a scientist's taste for hard inductive evidence over abstract assertion. Deirdre writes like a dream. Though completely comfortable with the expository requirements of scholarly writing, she is a natural stylist who expresses herself with grace and concision. It seemed only natural to me that her short stories were accepted for publication in the *Black Kettle Review*, a prestigious regional journal. As any professor will tell you, it is a rare thing to be able to say that one truly *enjoys* reading a student's papers. With Deirdre's papers, I can proudly and honestly say that.

- Marcus is very curious and analytical, and he has the intellectual versatility to develop new expertise quickly. Though he had no exposure to the gaming industry, in only his second year at CapitalBanc he wrote a white paper on Southeast Asia's resort, and gaming industry that earned him quite a reputation among our investment analysts. He found sources unknown to our industry analyst in Macau, identified Royal Mekong Partners as a company to watch even before its new Hai Phong casino was announced, and crafted a one-, five-, and ten-year investment scenario that management has been following to the letter. Generally, second-year analysts at CapitalBanc don't get the chance to present their white papers themselves, but I greenlighted Marcus's participation in a gaming industry investment conference in which he gave a poised presentation of his findings to industry folks 10 to 20 years his senior. He's now also exercising his literary gifts as a columnist for CapitalBanc's internal investment tip sheet, *Capital Ideas*. Marcus tells me that law schools seek analytically strong applicants who can write, research, and speak well. He is more skilled in these areas than any second-year analyst I've ever worked with.

Impact and Accomplishments

■ Jennifer's bachelor's project won both the Goolsbye Essay Prize and the University Provost Award—the first time I know of that both have been awarded to the same thesis. Jennifer's achievement was superlative in every respect. First, in terms of sheer length, she submitted a paper that was almost as long as some doctoral dissertations I've received, though she had only two semesters to work on it. Second, her research effort was extraordinary. Her bibliography alone ran to nine pages, including multiple texts in Russian and Japanese. Third, the quality of her writing, while hardly flawless, was better than that of any other senior thesis I've seen in my years at the university. Last and most importantly was the quality, originality, and maturity of her scholarship. Jennifer fashioned a nuanced and compelling case that the immediate cause of Japan's surrender in August 1945 was not, contrary to conventional wisdom, the atomic bombing of Hiroshima and Nagasaki but Russia's opening of a second front against the Kurile Islands and Hokkaido. For an undergraduate, indeed, for a student at almost any level, it was a tour de force. For that alone I am convinced that Jennifer will absolutely thrive in law school.

■ As Tom Heinz's supervising pastor, I can attest to the impact he has made at New Shiloh Baptist Church through his dedication, gift for counseling, and communication skills. Like our four other pastors-in-training, Tom is assigned to minister over 100 church members in activities ranging from pastoral visits to the homes of ill or needy congregants, leading a morning service and preaching two Sunday evening devotionals a month, counseling congregants with spiritual and personal issues during pastors' one-on-one hours, and working toward timely completion of his theological study project. Tom approaches all these responsibilities with a devotion I have rarely encountered in 20 years of pastoral work. He is at the pastor's office at 7:30 every morning and frequently stays until 7 or 8 at night. When one of our congregants lost his home and belongings in an apartment fire, Tom hosted him for two weeks while he found a new place. On his own initiative he has started a community outreach breakfast for teens on Saturdays that has tripled in attendance in only a year. He is enormously popular among our youngest congregants and always has time to shoot baskets with the boys from Highland School. When our senior pastor was briefly hospitalized last December, Tom offered to take on my entire pastoral counseling calendar (in addition to his own) while I stepped in for Reverend Gilchrist. Finally, Tom's skills as a preacher and biblical scholar are evident in the increasing mastery he shows in his Sunday devotionals, which have been among our best-attended services. At the same time, it's been obvious to all of us that since his wife's death in Iraq in 2006, Tom has felt deeply conflicted about the ministry and his true calling. Over the past 16 months Tom has tested, with his usual sense of commitment, his belief that pursuing his wife's planned career, as a public interest lawyer, will enable him to achieve greater impact than he can as a pastor. It's not for me to judge whether Tom is correct in that belief; but I can assure you that his ability to positively touch lives through his counsel, his concern, and his compassion is simply extraordinary.

■ Tim's organizational skills were the best of any intern we've had over the years and the equal of many employees. Before Tim's start date, the partners and I were talking about whether we had showed "favoritism" by awarding Tim the internship just because his father is a client. We decided to challenge Tim from the start with an assignment in which he would be given minimal instructions and less time than he would probably need: reviewing the compliance of all 30 of our shipping industry clients with New York state's documentation reporting requirements. We also asked Tim to scan and digitize these documents, so we could access key data quickly. Though we expected Tim would be unable to finish the project in his three months with us, he jumped on the assignment immediately and five weeks after his start date gave us a spreadsheet breakdown of each client's compliance status and a stack of indexed CD-ROMs. I had my secretary randomly sample Tim's work to see if he had rushed it, but she said it was meticulous and complete. I was even more impressed to learn that Tim had come in on some weekends to work on the project and had even resourcefully convinced two secretaries to do some of the scanning for him. Many young interns would have sloppily rushed through such a frankly monotonous project, but Tim did not. He has the attention to detail and thoroughness that all outstanding attorneys need.

Weaknesses

- Zhen is not without his faults, of course. I have seem him "pile on" a classmate during a heated class discussion when it's clear to everyone, including Zhen's interlocutor, that he's won his point. I don't consider this reflective of character flaws, however. As I've noted, Zhen is a warm and compassionate person. His occasional classroom victory laps are more a function of the "animal spirits" that go hand in hand with youth and immaturity. As Zhen encounters minds as supple and powerful as his own, which he will at Yale, he'll gain some humility and restraint.

- Cathy's intellect is as sharp as a switchblade. When she focuses it, she can analyze a problem as incisively as any student I've taught. Her weakness is her relative lack of perspective or the ability to place the problems she analyzes in a broader context. Lacking this "bigger picture"—primarily because she is still young and not widely read—she can in her interpretations lose the forest for the trees. The final result can be sophisticated linguistic exegesis but also counterintuitive or common sensically false. I regard this flaw as the least of Cathy's worries, however. With serious study, continual reading, and the simple passage of time, she will become better at contextualizing issues than any of us.

Conclusions

■ Brent is among the top five or six interns I have worked with in my three decades as a practicing attorney. In fact, the partners and I were so pleased with his performance that we offered him a departing bonus, something we've done only once before. I'm certain Brent will thrive in your program and enjoy a brilliant career in the law. I'd be happy to answer any questions you may have about Brent; please call me at (123) 555–7890.

■ If he chose to, Sachin could build an outstanding, even singular career for himself as a scholar of Canadian history. Indeed, I urged him more than once to seriously reconsider abandoning his Ph.D. work. But each time the reasons Sachin gave me for wanting to pursue a law degree were so thoughtful, concrete, and persuasive that I eventually stopped trying. Though the contribution he could make to history would I believe be substantial, he will likely make just as significant an impact in the law. I say that not because I am an expert in the law, but because I have recommended three students to the University of Chicago Law School who eventually earned J.D.s there, and Sachin's intellectual and language skills are at least as strong as theirs. He is without question among the top 1 percent of students I have worked with in my 25-year career. Feel free to contact me at [number or e-mail] if I can provide any more information about Sachin Bajpai.

Wait-List Letters

Introductions

- As a wait-listed applicant, I am writing to update the committee on the developments in my career since I applied in early November. I would also like to reiterate my strong commitment to earning a law degree at the University of Minnesota. In the past six months I have earned my master's degree in municipal finance, added substantial new achievements at Ernst & Young, and further reinforced my conviction that Minnesota Law is the ideal program for me.

- Thank you for your letter of April 21 explaining the admissions committee's decision to place my application in your reserve category. Though I have already returned the enclosed card indicating my commitment to remaining under consideration for admission to Boston University, I am writing to update the committee on recent developments that I believe strengthen my credentials.

- Being wait-listed at my first-choice law school is a bittersweet feeling. Though disappointed I did not make the "first cut," it is a relief to know that I can still hold out hope of joining the Georgetown class of 2012. I am writing to enclose an additional reference letter from a recommender who will add a new perspective on my candidacy, to affirm my deepening sense of fit with Georgetown following my most recent campus visit, and to assure you that I will immediately accept any offer of admission you extend to me.

New Developments

- Since applying, I have continued to gain skills that will serve me well as an attorney. In early December, my graduation from Syracuse University's master's program coincided with my AT Kearney team's completion of a $1.6 million ERP implementation at MetLife. In January, my Kearney manager formally recognized the management skills I gained at Syracuse—as well as the leadership and technical skills I've demonstrated in my consulting engagements—by recommending me to new client Dow Corning as a team lead for our first project with the company. After only two weeks at Dow Corning, my five-person team and I were able to meet the client's needs so precisely that it purchased over $300,000 in additional services from us. Based on this breakthrough, Kearney is promoting me to senior consultant on July 1. My recent engagements at Kearney have also reinforced my conviction that a legal education is absolutely essential to my achieving my professional goals.

- After submitting my application last November, I continued to work on John McCain's presidential campaign. Despite a shoestring budget, I am proud to have led volunteer teams in get-out-the-vote campaigns in four key states. Through strategic use of our limited advertising budget, we increased the senator's name recognition, achieved substantial increases in contribution rates, and secured endorsements from key community leaders. Most remarkable was our staff's ability to leverage the astonishing (albeit unpredictable) power of the Internet in deploying innovative Web strategies that registered over 130,000 supporters online and raised nearly $10 million in small donations in a matter of weeks. I believe these efforts were essential to Senator McCain's ability to achieve the come-from-behind victories in February and March 2008 that even we loyalists considered far-fetched the previous summer. After the senator became the presumptive Republican nominee on March 4, I began coordinating the integration of informal McCain grassroots groups to create a better command structure for the months leading up to and following the Republican National Convention. My familiarity with the structure of George W. Bush's organizations in 2004 is enabling me to reform the legal classification, local and national framework, and mission statements of many of Senator McCain's grassroots organizations. I believe these unusually enriching experiences will deepen the contribution I can make to my Stanford Law class.

- Though I applied to William and Mary only two months ago I have continued to refine my skills and learn more about the law. Since November, for example, I have been helping two partners at Malraux, Archie & Donovan in the acquisition and permitting of an $8 million warehouse property in Fort Lauderdale. Working on the challenging transactional paperwork involving land use and zoning restrictions, construction, redevelopment, and financing has intensified my fascination with real estate law. The partners I reported to were so pleased with my work that they assigned me due diligence work on the property's title and environmental reports, which are not normally handled by law clerks. In fact, I'm the only clerk who has been allowed to fly to Tallahassee on her own to review title commitments and land surveys at the Land Use and Environmental Services Division and other state offices. It's been an exciting few months and has solidified my interest in specializing in real estate law.

Reaffirmation of School Fit

- The rapid convergence of Internet technology and politics is creating a new professional niche for legal counsel who can advise candidates on the risks and rewards of "cyber politics." As I explained in my personal statement last November, my varied experience as the

187

Internet chief of staff for a major presidential candidate, two years' experience in Google's marketing group, and an undergraduate double major in telecommunications and political science have uniquely prepared me to fill this niche. The missing piece remains a J.D. All my experiences since applying have confirmed my conviction that Georgetown Law Center is the ideal J.D. program for my needs. It offers me the unique breadth of Curriculum B and the unique focus of the Intellectual Property, Entertainment, and Technology Law cluster as well as directly relevant student clubs like the Republican Law Students Association and Georgetown Law Militia and journals like *Georgetown Journal of Law and Public Policy*. Not least, living in the nation's capital will give me ready access to the levers of political power and convenient proximity to the heart of New Media power: New York City. The more I have learned about Georgetown since applying, the more certain I feel that it is my first and only choice for law school.

■ The University of Pennsylvania Law School is, more than ever, my top choice. In early April, I traveled to Philadelphia to revisit the school and meet with student friends like Li Zhou (J.D., 2010) and Raul Levereau (J.D., 2009). While sitting in on Dr. Kreimer's constitutional law class, I felt the incredible sense of community that Li and Raul have assured me Penn has institutionalized through its section system and abandonment of class rank and GPAs. I was the recipient of a vivid example of that community when my first-year host, Janice Berline, floored me by offering to help me find an apartment, despite the fact that she was in the middle of preparing for test blocks! Even Dr. Kreimer emanated a warm, approachable style in the inclusive way he taught the class (easily the most engrossing I've sat in on). I left Philadelphia determined to do my best to convince you, the admissions committee, that no other law program can provide me what Penn Law can.

■ After three campus visits and conversations with twelve Arizona Law students I thought I had uncovered every relevant reason for making the University of Arizona Rogers College of Law my first choice. Then I spoke last week with second-year students Zeke Juarez and Mariko Thomas. They pointed out that Arizona's Courtroom of the Future and Law Office of the Future projects will help me master law-related technologies that will only grow increasingly relevant to exhibit presentation in the years to come—thus making them a key component in my goal of building a reputation as a specialist in juror decision making. Just as practically, Arizona's judicial clerking program and Fegtly Moot Court Competitions will polish my lawyering skills to a fine luster while dovetailing nicely with the work I hope to do under Professor Bublick on appellate and trial court litigation. Similarly, at Arizona I can explore the increasingly fertile nexus of law and psychology by studying with Professors Gottfredson, Sales, and Mauet.

Conclusions

■ Finally, I am enclosing a letter of recommendation from Dr. Erol Birnbaum, who became my instructor in the Red Cross's Future Leadership program three years ago. When I graduated from that program last June, Dr. Birnbaum honored me by nominating me to the board of directors of the Nashville Red Cross. I hope Dr. Birnbaum's letter will shed new light on the commitment to community that I'm excited about continuing through Cornell's live-client legal aid clinic. I would be happy to provide any other information that might help the committee reach a positive decision on my candidacy.

■ I believe the University of Florida is entitled to expect a return on the investment I am asking it to make in me. As evidence of my contribution, I offer my intensive exposure to two cultures—Vietnam and the United States—which has given me a sensitivity to the impact of cultural differences on economic and legal issues. I also offer the unusual breadth of my professional experiences, which range from management consulting and investment banking to estate planning law. Finally, I offer the creativity reflected in my film and literary work, which I will dedicate to enriching my Levin classmates' learning experience. I'm excited about joining all of them in "stepping up the stairs" toward a challenging and rewarding career in tax law. I remain hopeful that UF Law will agree with me that the Levin School is truly where I belong. Thank you for your continued consideration of my candidacy.

- Ms. Jimenez, please be assured that if Temple University Beasley School of Law offers me admission, I will enthusiastically and immediately accept. By combining my rigorous background in business and technology with the legal foundation I gain at Temple, the next time an entrepreneur asks for my help, I will have all the tools I need to give it. I look forward to learning of your decision.

Part IV

Perfect Phrases for Law School Admissions Interviews

Chapter 12 Perfect Phrases for Law School Interviews

Although most law schools do not offer formal interviews as part of the application process, the number that do is growing. More importantly, even law schools that do not formally interview applicants are usually more than happy to talk with them informally, and not just via anonymous exchanges at crowded school information events. So-called stealth interviews, sometimes with the admissions director himself or herself, can often be arranged if you inquire proactively and appropriately. If you fail to exploit this major loophole in law schools'"no interviews" policy, you will not have done all you can to maximize your chances of being admitted. Let's review some perfect phrases for some of the most common interview questions.

"Tell me about yourself."

■ Sure. Though I was born and raised in Peoria, Illinois, I think I can say I've led a pretty unusual life. When I was 10, my father took a sabbatical from his teaching job and bought a sailboat, which he and my mother, sister, and I sailed around the Caribbean for two years. The exposure I gained to the cultural variety of that region was an incredible revelation for me, and ever since then I have been a travel and language nut. So far I've lived or worked in four countries, including Norway, Panama, and the United Kingdom, and I speak three languages fluently: English, Norwegian, and German. I think I can offer a lot in terms of cross-cultural insights to my Yale classmates. When I was 16, my family moved to Oslo, Norway, which was a bit difficult for me at first because of the cold winters and language barrier. I worked hard at learning the language though and eventually made friends who showed me Scandinavia's hot spots and backpacked with me through Europe, including Russia. My interest in international law grew directly from these unusual experiences. Some of my Norwegian friends were interested in opening a Häagen-Dazs franchise in Trondheim and wondered which laws would govern a franchising agreement for a U.S. company in Norway. I wanted to help them and began researching the differences between the two countries' franchise disclosure laws, agency/principal rules, and so on. I actually helped them during their initial negotiations with Häagen-Dazs's headquarters in Minnesota. While earning my accounting degree at Northwestern, I took electives in international trade and international finance and spent my summers getting internship experience with Chicago-based companies that have big international markets: Kraft Foods for one summer, Boeing for two. I want to be corporate counsel for one of these firms, which is why I'm here today.

"Why did you decide to go to [name] University for your undergraduate degree?"

■ Well, I guess you could say I initially picked UC Santa Barbara for all the "wrong" reasons—like the weather, the ocean, and being near Los Angeles. My family vacationed there summers when I was growing up, and I really loved the lifestyle. I also felt a little claustrophobic in Batesville. Living in Santa Barbara was even better than I imagined, but I didn't hit the books as much as I should have my first year. I was fortunate to take a course in Japanese literature with Professor John Nathan my second year, however, and that really gave me focus. I fell in love with the works of Kenzaburo Oe and Yukio Mishima, started learning Japanese, spent a year studying at Keio University in Tokyo, and became a leader of the UCSB Japanese Student Association. UC Santa Barbara has a well-earned reputation as a party school, but when I "got serious" my sophomore year, it had all the resources I needed.

■ My high school was the typical American suburban high school where jocks and conformity rule and intellectual, creative, or unusual people—like me—were considered "nerds" and social outcasts. Without really being conscious of it, I think I looked for a university where I would feel at home with other people like me. I made visits to a couple of Big Ten campuses but didn't really feel that they were different from my high school environment. I still remember the day I toured the University of Chicago's campus in Hyde Park with my dad. The guy who showed us around was an articulate, bespectacled type, sort of nerdy but with attitude—my type. And the campus itself is full of Oxford or Cambridge-style architecture, so it appealed to my desire for something a little different. As an early-decision applicant, I applied to no other schools and never regretted that decision. It's true that I struggled a little academically at first, but that was just because I needed to adjust to the rigor of the education Chicago gives you.

I eventually graduated with honors. More importantly, in my four years at Chicago I met wonderfully interesting and intelligent people from every part of the world, challenged myself intellectually like I never had before, and discovered my interest in economic theory.

"Tell me about your job [or internship or thesis]."

■ I've spent the two years since college graduation working for LawnZone.com, a Web-based one-stop shop for lawn-care products, services, and information. I was hired into the human resources department and had a lot of involvement in our customer service initiatives. Last year customer complaints about rudely answered calls and delayed orders began spiking, so my boss sent me to Sioux Rapids, Iowa, in May to get our customer service representatives in line. The CSRs were rural whites with no formal education beyond high school and an average age of 38. I was the young, inexperienced African American from Boston with a graduate degree. So it was interesting at first. Instead of issuing orders, I grabbed one of the empty cubicles and began listening in on customer calls, processing applications along with the reps, ordering a lot of pizzas for delivery, and letting the CSRs talk in anything-goes meetings. I told them honestly which of their suggestions might fly, like avoiding call scripts, and which ones I thought headquarters would ding. By being transparent to them, I won their trust and was able to get them to accept performance metrics and defined objectives in exchange for new incentives. Our customer service satisfaction scores are up by 80 percent, and I was promoted in August to Special Projects. This experience is also what made me think seriously about getting a J.D. in labor law.

■ I studied incidences of depression among female students at four colleges in Ontario, Canada, under a grant from the Mental Health Commission of Canada. My mother was an alcoholic and manic-depressive so I've always been interested in mental health issues. I majored in psychology at the University of Toronto and wrote a historical survey of alternatives to the Beck Depression Inventory for Dr. Ewing Dray. He suggested that I make student mental health the subject of my senior thesis. I decided to focus on female students to make the data analysis challenge more manageable and because my preliminary research on the literature indicated that depression might be more prevalent among women. With the help of a friend, I administered the Beck Depression Inventory test to 630 students at

➡

the four campuses over four months. After sorting and analyzing the valid surveys, I found that 34 percent of the sample indicated clinical ranges of depression and that 15 percent had considered suicide—even higher than I had expected. I found that the numbers were even higher among international female students—close to 40 percent and 20 percent, respectively. My findings had a major impact on me personally and professionally. Personally, my sister is starting college next year, and I worry about her. Professionally, I want to lead a mental health-related NGO such as the National Alliance on Mental Illness, Carter Center's Mental Health Program, or the World Federation for Mental Health.

"Why do you want to go to law school? What type of law do you want to practice?"

■ As a junior examiner and then primary patent examiner at the U.S. Patent and Trademark Office, I have been applying statutory (Title 35) and case law to the examination of telecommunications-related patent applications for four years now. Law school will give me the practical and theoretical expertise to leverage my PTO and telecommunications engineering background to begin a career in intellectual property law. In the short term, a J.D. in IP with an emphasis in patent law will help me become a more effective and productive patent examiner. In the longer term, it will enable me to work as a patent attorney representing clients in interference proceedings or bringing patent-related lawsuits to federal court as well as defending them. Alternatively, I may stay with the PTO and become a patent judge at the board of appeals.

■ I majored in accounting at Stanford University. Out of curiosity, in my senior year I took a business law elective taught by Professor Charles Meyers, which discussed the U.S. Bankruptcy Code (Title 11) and famous tort-related bankruptcies like Johns-Manville, Dow Corning, and Texaco. I wrote a paper on the early history of composition agreements that was well-received, and that basically planted the seed. During law school I hope to clerk for a summer with a major bankruptcy boutique firm such as Friedman Dumas & Springwater or McNutt & Litteneker. After law school I'd like to clerk for a bankruptcy judge so I can understand bankruptcy law through his or her eyes—what judges think works, what gets on their nerves, etc. Ultimately, I want to establish a solo practice representing secured creditors like insurance companies and banks in Chapter 11 cases. I'm attracted to the mix of litigation and

➡

transaction work that bankruptcy law entails and the range of laws it touches, from tax issues and contracts to loans and leases.

"Why would a [nontraditional prelaw professional] want to go to law school?"

- As my college graduation approached, I realized that my passion for athletics was still far stronger than my interest in any conventional career tracks, so I decided to accept my university's offer to become coach of its women's softball team. During my tenure, my softball team rewrote school and conference record books and won its first conference championship. I personally coached our nationally ranked pitching staff, whose honors included NFCA All-American scholar athletes, conference pitcher of the year, and the first perfect game and no-hitters in school history. Through coaching, I learned how to hone others' skills, how to be assertive, how to provide instructions that are detailed yet brief enough for 17- to–22-year-olds to take in. Coaching also developed my organizational skills, both mental and physical. I juggled multiple functions simultaneously, including organizing complex logistical events like a team trip to Hawaii, where I coordinated travel schedules, game times, recreational activities, and group meals. Finally, coaching developed my interpretive and advocacy skills. To effectively argue your position in a disputed call with an umpire, you need to have a clear grasp of the rules and their various interpretations. I know umpire's "rulings" are rarely overturned, but to sustain my credibility as an advocate I still had to know the game's "statutory law" down to the smallest subsubsection. When my attorney father died suddenly in 2007, I agreed to help my brother, a Tulane J.D., organize my father's office and files. Over four months, I got a crash course in the life of a solo practitioner, and I was intrigued. I was especially interested in his personal injury and product liability work, disciplines I had sometimes encountered as a coach soothing the angry parents' of injured athletes. As my brother took over my father's practice, I became his informal second in command and glorified paralegal. We experienced the challenges and triumphs of keeping my father's legacy afloat together. It was exhilarating. Those seven months taught me a lot, including that the law is the only thing I've found that matches my passion for college coaching.

■ Well, in college I was definitely the "invisible hand," free-enterprise type. I wrote for Bowdoin's student libertarian paper and worked for Michael Badnarik's

2004 presidential campaign. As a latter-day Adam Smith I believed that economies should be allowed to allocate resources without government interference since the working out of their own inner logic creates the greatest efficiencies. Soon after I joined Bain Consulting, however, my passion for open markets collided with my humanity. In my first project I was assigned to determine the optimal manufacturing footprint for a global consumer electronics manufacturer. To gather data, my team and I visited facilities in Bulgaria, the Philippines, and the United States, ultimately developing a complex model that optimized the client's total costs. Not surprisingly, manufacturing products in the U.S. was clearly cost-ineffective, and the "inner logic" of our analysis produced a recommendation to downsize over 5,000 U.S. workers. Our plan would significantly improve profitability for our clients but put hundreds of people out of work, many of whom I'd met during plant tours. I began to really question my "unfettered market forces" philosophy. I guess you could say that I had a conversion experience. The role of the government in refining the market's brute logic, in restraining its raw impulses, became compelling to me. A law degree will enable me to join a federal agency such as the Federal Trade Commission or the legislative staff of a congressional committee where the "visible hand" of government is controlled.

"Why do you want to attend our law school?"

■ I'd be lying if I said that Vanderbilt's reputation wasn't a factor in my attraction. I'm from Tennessee, but I'm open to practicing anywhere in the South or in Washington, D.C., and I want to study law with people from all over. So Vanderbilt's national class profile and placement are important to me. But my real interest in Vanderbilt goes back to my father's attorney, Charlie Knight, who earned his J.D. at Vanderbilt in 1965. Charlie was an old-school, jack-of-all-trades attorney who got to know his clients as friends and handled almost everything for them, from wills and estate planning to contracts, family law, and property. He did it all and was sort of a grandfather figure to me, letting me shadow him in college and helping me out of a couple of youthful scrapes I got into. He sang Vanderbilt's praises all the time and would have been delighted to know it's my first-choice school. Of course, Vanderbilt's probably changed a lot since Charlie's time, but I know its tradition as the first law school to launch a law and business program is alive and directly aligns with my plans to pursue corporate law with a large firm.
I intend to enroll in the Law and Business certificate program, join in the Business Law Society, and participate in the Business Law Clinic. Classes like "Mergers and Acquisitions Deal Dynamics" and "Law and Finance of

Equity Markets" are right up my alley. I appreciate that Vandy's a small program, because I'm the kind of person, like Charlie, who likes to get to know people, personalize relationships, and build long-term networks. Finally, I'm also a country-and-western fan, so living in Nashville is sort of like dying and going to heaven.

- Unlike other law schools that only claim to be interdisciplinary, NYU School of Law truly offers tremendous interdisciplinary study and research opportunities. The Engelberg Center on Innovation Law and Policy and such colloquia as "Law, Philosophy and Political Theory" and "Rational Choice, Legal Institutions, and Political Organizations" will enhance my own interdisciplinary approach to the law, which encompasses political science, history, economics, and ethics. I believe this diverse perspective will enable me to enrich class discussion and contribute to the success of your students and your program. My research into biotechnology and political science has also exposed me to the fine scholarship of NYU's faculty, from Professor Ronald Dworkin's book *Life's Dominion* and Professor Richard L. Revesz's articles on federalism and environmental protection to Professor Michael Ferejohn's coedited study *The New Federalism—Can the States Be Trusted?* To get to know these scholars personally would be extremely rewarding for me.

"What other schools are you applying to?"

- Because Boston is where I intend to practice, I've applied to Boston College, Boston University, and Northeastern University. All are fine schools with many of the resources I need, but BC is head and shoulders above in the areas that matter most to me: its range of clinical programs, its yearlong writing class, and the overseas opportunities with the Holocaust/Human Rights Project and International Criminal Tribunal. To be honest, I'm also a somewhat liberal-leaning Catholic, so BC's Catholic Jesuit tradition matters to me too.

"Why should we accept you? What would you add to our program?"

- Well, aside from my competitive numbers, I think I can bring a pretty diverse perspective to my classmates that will really enhance their law school experience. Professionally, I have unusual leadership exposure to both the public and private sectors. As the commander of gunnery crews on a U.S. Navy frigate, for example, I was exposed to the unique technical and leadership demands of a military unit at sea. Later I gained an entirely different perspective serving as an operational facilitator/liaison for the Naval District Legal Service Office (the navy's judge advocate general) in Washington, D.C. That sparked my interest in a career in the law, but I wanted to give the private sector a fair shake, so I joined Flextronics for a year and a half, deciding in the end that the outsourced electronics manufacturing industry wasn't for me. On the personal side, I can offer the insights of someone who has led effectively in the U.S. Navy, which is a real "rainbow coalition" in terms of ethnicity, gender, and geographical origin. As someone who's part Native, Irish, and Korean American, I guess I would be considered a "diversity" applicant. But as an avid scuba diver I also bring a unique vision of the global community. Scuba diving opens up an entire "global community" of natural life that most people never experience. I've found that diving with people creates bridges across cultural and language differences as we explore the diversity of the underwater world that binds everyone on earth. My family's story and my acting and directing experiences with the Pacific Rim Shakespeare Festival add to the contribution I can bring to Chicago Law, and I'd be glad to talk about them.

"Tell me about a legal issue that's important to you."

■ I've always been fascinated by the way discussions of the Second Amendment—"A well regulated militia being necessary to the security of a free State, the right of the People to keep and bear arms, shall not be infringed"—quickly dissolve into litmus tests of one's membership in the "strict constructionist" or "judicial activist" schools. I also find it fascinating that the Supreme Court has until recently avoided directly addressing the central question of the Second Amendment: does it give Americans a basic individual right to bear arms or only a collective right as members of a militia? On the one hand, I grant it's significant that from the Bill of Rights' ratification to the early twentieth century, courts mostly assumed that the Second Amendment did confer an individual right to bear arms. And I agree that it would have been inconsistent for the Founders to use the term "the People" in the collective sense in this amendment when they used it in the individual sense in the other nine. On the other hand, I believe the Court majorities in *Presser v. Illinois* and *U.S. v. Miller* got it right: that (respectively) *states* may infringe the right to bear arms and that possessing a firearm as an individual is not protected in the same way as possessing a firearm used in one's role as a

➡

militia member "acting in concert for the common defense." Finally, I'm uncomfortable with the idea that Americans' constitutional rights should be defined in perpetuity by the world-view and the "intent" of individuals who countenanced slavery and the denial of women's suffrage.

- In 1996, Congress passed the Defense of Marriage Act, or DOMA, which defines marriage for purposes of all federal laws as a legal union between one man and one woman and declares that states need not recognize a marriage from another state if it is between persons of the same sex. Today, 45 states have either a constitutional amendment or statute defining marriage as a union between a man and a woman. DOMA matters to me because as a gay man I am unprotected by the law and subject to legal and tax liabilities that married persons do not encounter. For example, estate tax rates for unmarried individuals range from 37 to 55 percent for total taxable estates, whereas for traditional married couples the surviving partner receives an unlimited marital deduction. The same goes for the gift tax. While married couples can give each other any amount tax-free while they're alive, gay couples face restrictive limits. Similarly, I must have a durable medical power of attorney in place so the person I— but not the law—consider to be my spouse can make medical decisions if I am unable to express my preferences. DOMA is the reason I want to earn the J.D. As an attorney practicing family law, I will be able to assist my clients with estate planning and domestic partner agreements. I will also be able to defend gay couples facing relationship breakups; for these couples divorce laws that oversee the distribution of assets between married individuals do not apply. Given the law's silence on nontraditional couples, I can also help them arrange amicable child custody and visitation agreements.

"What's a good book you've read recently?"

■ I've been recommending Michael Pollan's *The Omnivore's Dilemma* as a must-read for anyone who enjoys food. It tells the "natural history" of four meals—following them from our dinner plates back to their natural (and unnatural) sources. One of the meals is a typical fast-food meal, which turns out to be mostly made of corn; the second is a meal comprised of the semiorganic or "industrial" organic foods that are sold at national organic grocery chains; the third consists of food from strictly local organic farms; and the fourth is a meal

⟶

hunted and gathered by Pollard himself. It's an informative, thought-provoking book, and one that's directly related to the health-related legislation I hope to work on as a congressional committee staff attorney. As someone who's done some freelance journalism I really admire Pollard's writing—lucid, personal, funny, and sometimes moving. My fiancée said the book made her question why she eats certain foods, like corn and chicken. But it made me hungry! When I finished it, I took her out to eat at a really good restaurant—vegetarian.

- I'm a big fan of the Library of America series. I have about 10 of the volumes, and the one I've enjoyed most is the second Lincoln volume, which covers the last seven years of his life and his presidency. I grew up in southern Illinois, which is Lincoln country, so we memorized the Gettysburg Address in high school and studied his "greatest hits." But in reading this collection straight through recently, I realized what a great writer Lincoln really was. "The occasion is piled high with difficulty and we must rise with the occasion. As our case is new, so we must think anew and act anew. We must disenthrall ourselves and then we will save our country." That always gives me goosebumps, and it's typical of Lincoln's direct, "ordinary" but powerful language. Because the book includes letters as well as speeches, it also shows Lincoln's day-by-day concerns and his folksy intellect. The only other thing I've memorized is his note to General Grant in 1864: "Hold on with a bull-dog grip, and chew and choke as much as possible." I love that. Also, of course, Lincoln was a lawyer, and a very good one. He was one of the early inspirations behind my decision to become one too.

"Could you explain this gap of six months on your résumé in 2008?"

■ Sure. As you know, the subprime crisis led to Bear Stearns' purchase for pennies by Morgan Stanley, and in April, my entire department was downsized—15 people in all. As the credit markets were still reeling, most of the companies I would have looked to for work were not hiring. I interviewed at over 20 firms in the space of six months, networked at at least 10 industry events and conferences, and used my personal network to do informational interviews outside the industry. But the economy wasn't being very friendly to job hunters. Fortunately, I also used my time between jobs to deepen my involvement at The Hope Place, mentoring two kids, who are now my good buddies, and earning an invitation to join its board. Seeing how a nonprofit works from the top down was really a mind-blowing experience for me. First, I saw how resourceful and creative it has to be to find funding and what kind of obstacles—for example, regulatory issues, staff turnover, competition with other nonprofits for fund-raising dollars—it has to deal with. Second, I saw how dedicated and talented my fellow board members were. These were MBAs and J.D.s who really cared about what The Hope Place was about. One of the lawyers, Linda Bodega, kind of took me under her wing and encouraged me to sink my teeth into the organization more than I had planned to—I was actually working as a full-time volunteer for The Hope Place at that point. Before I knew it, Linda was connecting me with her network in Bridgeport's legal and nonprofit community, and by October she had lined up the funding for me to become a paid staff administrator for The Hope Place. I am fully committed to leading nonprofits as my career and—given the strong skills I already have in finance—believe a J.D. is the degree that will enable me to achieve that goal.

"How do you account for the discrepancy between your GPA and LSAT score?"

■ I'm glad you asked that because I believe the explanation will convince you that my 169 LSAT score is the "real me." In high school I was covaledictorian and recipient of an academic scholarship to the university of my choice. My divorced mother couldn't contribute to my college tuition, so after my first year at Kansas University I planned to get a part-time job to cover my expenses beyond my scholarship. Then, in the spring of freshman year my mother was diagnosed with fibroid tumors, and I had to return to Carbondale to oversee her surgery and recovery. Since my mother didn't have the resources to survive without her job, I increased my school-year work schedule to full-time, and basically supported myself and my mother for the rest of my college years. My GPA had been 3.8 when my mother became ill, and though I was able to establish a rising GPA trend in my remaining years, the full-time job really took a toll on my grades. But I'm actually proud of the sense of responsibility and priority I showed in choosing to take on a full-time job—I believe family comes first. I successfully petitioned to keep my academic scholarship, and the skills I gained working at Archer Daniels Midland gave me a huge advantage

➡

when I joined the workforce after graduation. On the strength of my work history, recommendations, and interview skills, I was able to overcome my GPA and land a coveted management trainee position with Cargill, which is where I developed my interest in agricultural law.

- There's always been a "disconnect" between my performance on standardized tests and my academic performance. For example, my SAT score was a 920, yet my cumulative GPA in high school was a 3.8, and I was accepted into both the National Honor Society and the Chinese National Honor Society because of my grades. Despite my low SAT score, I was accepted into Emory University based on my extracurricular activities and my GPA, and I proved that my SAT was not predictive by achieving a cumulative 3.4 undergraduate GPA, including dean's list for five semesters. Similarly, though I scored a 151 on the LSAT, I earned an A in a postbacc legal theory course at Columbia University, and in my professional career I have earned three promotions in two years and routinely do the work of lawyers for at the fifth-largest law firm in New Jersey.

"Do you have any questions for me?"

- "Is the new dean planning any major changes that will affect next year's entering class?"
- "What are the opportunities for students to get involved in or help out in the admissions process?"
- "What do you think are the greatest misconceptions applicants have about the law school?"
- "I was impressed by your great placement rate for federal clerkships. Are there particular judges or circuits that you have strong relationships with?"

Closing Thoughts

Though a 179 LSAT score may come close, there are in reality no magic bullets to law school admission. Even high-index-number applicants can trip themselves up with an immature, pompous personal statement. At the end of the day, what you (and others) write and say about yourself in your application file will play a huge role in your odds of success. And the words that succeed are usually the ones backed up with the most honesty, self-knowledge, creativity, and hard work.

Remember this as you consult this and other admissions guidebooks. Admissions officers read books like these too, and they have an uncanny ability (honed on the job) to recall passages they've encountered before. More importantly, they have an uncanny ability to detect when an applicant's essay rings false. For these reasons alone, do yourself a favor and use this book's "ready-to-use" phrases only as models to study, inspirations to emulate, or even first-draft crutches on the way to your own voice. Because in the end, the only perfect phrase is your own.

Bibliography

Abrams, Lisa L., *The Official Guide to Legal Specialties* (Chicago: BarBri Group, 2000).

Bodine, Paul, *Great Personal Statements for Law School* (New York: McGraw-Hill, 2006).

Estrich, Susan, *How to Get into Law School* (New York: Riverhead Books, 2004).

Harvard Crimson staff, eds., *Fifty-five Successful Harvard Law School Application Essays* (New York: St. Martin's Griffin, 2007).

Ivey, Anna, *The Ivey Guide to Law School Admissions* (Orlando: Harcourt, 2005).

Martinson, Thomas H., and David P. Waldherr, *Getting into Law School Today*, 3d ed. (New York: Macmillan, 1998).

McGrath, Anne, and staff of U.S. News, eds., *Ultimate Guide to Law Schools*, 2d ed. (Naperville, IL: SourceBooks, Inc., 2006).

Montauk, Richard, *How to Get into the Top Law Schools*, rev. ed. (Paramus, NJ: Prentice Hall Press, 2006).

Wise, Carolyn C., and staff of Vault, eds., *The Law School Buzz Book,* 3d ed. (New York: Vault Inc., 2006).

About the Author

Paul Bodine is the author of *Great Personal Statements for Law School*, *Great Application Essays for Business School*, *Perfect Phrases for Business School Acceptance*, and *Perfect Phrases for Medical School Acceptance*. One of America's most experienced admissions consultants (serving clients since 1997), his clients have earned admission to such elite law schools as Harvard, Columbia, New York University, Virginia, Duke, Northwestern, Cornell, Georgetown, and Vanderbilt. A graduate of the University of Chicago and Johns Hopkins University, he lives in Southern California.